Political Behavior of the American Electorate

Sixth Edition

☆☆☆

William H. Flanigan
University of Minnesota

Nancy H. Zingale
College of St. Thomas

Allyn and Bacon, Inc.
Boston • London • Sydney • Toronto

To
Ruth M. and Edwin N. Flanigan
Amy K. Hill
and to the memory of
James S. Hill

Library of Congress Cataloging-in-Publication Data

Flanigan, William H.
  Political behavior of the American electorate.

  Includes bibliographical references and index.
  1. Voting—United States. I. Zingale, Nancy H.
II. Title.
JK1967.F38 1987   324.973   86-10949
ISBN 0-205-10342-1 (pbk.)

Series editor: *Judith Shaw*
Production coordinator: *Helyn Pultz*
Editorial-production service: *TKM Productions*
Cover coordinator: *Linda Dickinson*
Cover designer: *Susan Hamant*

Printed in the United States of America

10 9 8 7 6 5 4 3 2   90 89 88 87

Contents

$$\star\star\star$$

Acknowledgments   vii

Introduction   ix

1 ☆ Suffrage and Turnout   1

Extensions of Suffrage   2

Restrictions on Suffrage   4

The Eligible Electorate   6

Turnout in American Elections   8

"High Stimulus" and "Low Stimulus" Elections   13

Voters and Nonvoters   16

2 ☆ Partisanship   25

Party Loyalty   25

Party Identification   28

Independents: Are They Apolitical?   42

3 ☆ Social Characteristics of Partisans and Independents 49

The Social Composition of Partisan Groups 52
Social Group Analysis 55
Social Cross-Pressures 65

4 ☆ Partisan Change 69

Expected Voting Patterns 70
Types of Electoral Change 70
Party Systems and Major Realignments in American History 74
Partisan Change 81

5 ☆ Public Opinion and Ideology 93

Public Opinion on Political Issues 94
Issue Positions and Partisanship 96
Domestic Economic Issues 99
Social and Racial Issues 102
Foreign Affairs 106
Political Ideology 110
Ideological Identification 115

6 ☆ Vote Choice and Electoral Decisions 121

Candidate Image 122
Selling Presidential Candidates 125
Party Images 128
Issue Impact 132
Determinants of Vote Choice 140
Meaning of an Election 144

7 ☆ **Political Communication and Campaigns** **147**

Functions of Opinions for Individuals   148
Opinion Consistency and Dissonance   149
Political Communication   150
Political Campaigns   154
Campaign Participation and Its Impact   154
Mass Media and Election Campaigns   157
Impact of Election Campaigns   165
Campaign Strategy   168

8 ☆ **Political Culture and Socialization**   **171**

Democratic Beliefs and Values   172
Childhood Socialization   176
Citizen Roles and System Support   179
Protest and Violence   184

Appendix A
Survey Research Methods   **189**

Appendix B
Aggregate Election Statistics   **199**

Index   **205**

Acknowledgments

$$\star\ \star\ \star$$

The following analysis and description of the American electorate depends heavily on the work of others. Until 1960, extensive analysis of the research findings and data collected by social scientists was limited to an examination of published tables, but there have been significant changes since then. The major studies of American public opinion and voting behavior are now available to scholars throughout the world for further analysis and examination.

These developments in political analysis resulted from the cooperation of many individuals, but the efforts of two men associated with the Institute for Social Research at the University of Michigan deserve special mention. For a number of years the late Angus Campbell opened the archives of the Survey Research Center to outside scholars. This book has drawn on the work of many of the scholars who have benefited from this generosity. Warren Miller of the Center for Political Studies directed the organization and expansion of these archival activities through the creation of the Inter-university Consortium for Political and Social Research. The Consortium, composed of Michigan's Center for Political Studies and about 200 departments of political science, has made available to a wide clientele not only the archives of the Survey Research Center and the Center for Political Studies but other major data collections as well. Recognition of the benefits that this work has provided for scholars in tne fiela of political behavior has taken many forms. Most significantly, the National Science Foundation has begun continuous funding of the biennial election surveys.

This book is highly dependent on the Inter-university Consortium for Political and Social Research, both for large quantities of material collected by the Center for Political Stuaies and for election returns provided by the Historical Archive. We are pleased to acknowledge our great debt to the individuals in both organizations who have contributed to the establishment of these resources and services. We must hasten to add that neither the Center for Political Studies nor the Consortium bears any responsibility for the analysis and interpretations presented here. Indeed, the hazard of their efforts in providing open archives is the sort of reinterpretation and reanalysis that follows, and we can only hope that the weaknesses of this work will not reflect on the general worthiness and excellence of the Consortium and the Center.

We also wish to thank the many graduate and undergraduate students at the University of Minnesota who, over the years, have helped us with the analysis. Again, these acknowledgments do not diminish our responsibility for the errors that follow, but they qualify considerably the credit we are due.

W. H. F.
N. H. Z.

Introduction

$$\text{☆ ☆ ☆}$$

The first edition of this book was written in 1967. The plan of the book then, as now, was to present basic analysis and generalizations about the political behavior of Americans, illustrating and documenting these generalizations with the best survey data available. What was unknowable at the time was that the American polity was beginning a decade of political trauma. Not only would some basic changes in political life take place, but these changes would call into question some of the things political scientists thought they knew about the way Americans behave politically. The 1980s are (so far) a quieter time, but the awareness of change remains. Indeed, many of the trends that began or were accelerated by the crises of the late 1960s and early 1970s are only now tapering off, and whether this deceleration is permanent or temporary is as yet uncertain.

In this edition, we continue to focus attention on the major concepts and characteristics that shape Americans' responses to politics: Who votes and why? How does partisanship affect one's political behavior? How do economic and social characteristics influence people's politics? How do party loyalties, candidates' personalities, and issues affect the political choices we make? How much influence do the mass media have on our choices among candidates? Are Americans committed to upholding basic democratic values?

We will try to place the answers to these and other questions in the context of the changes that have occurred in American political behavior over the past twenty years. Specifically, we are concerned with the declining trend in voter turnout, the decline in the attachment to political parties, and the loss of trust by citizens for their government. These trends have all been the subject of much discussion by political analysts and commentators as to their meaning for future prospects for American democracy. Wherever possible, we try to put these recent trends in the broader context of political change over the 200 years of the republic.

The remainder of this introduction is a brief bibliographic review of the major works in the areas of elections, voting, and public opinion.

Major Voting Studies

The first important study of voting behavior and political opinion that relied on survey research techniques was directed by Paul Lazarsfeld, who was interested in the impact of mass media on individual vote choice during a presidential campaign. Lazarsfeld selected a single community, Erie County in Ohio, for his study of the 1940 presidential campaign. The publication of his findings, *The People's Choice*,[1] marked a milestone in social analysis. In 1948, Lazarsfeld, Bernard Berelson, and William McPhee of the Bureau of Applied Social Research at Columbia University conducted a second political study in Elmira, New York, and then published their findings in *Voting*.[2] Several major generalizations in political research emerged from these two studies: the cross-pressure hypothesis, opinion leadership, and selective perception. Up to this point the important public-opinion studies sampled single communities and were conducted entirely by sociologists.

In 1948, the newspaper polls predicted a Republican victory in the Dewey-Truman race for president, while a national survey conducted by the Survey Research Center at the University of Michigan showed Truman winning, publicizing the more scientific sampling

---

[1]Paul Lazarsfeld, Bernard Berelson, and Hazel Gaudet, *The People's Choice* (New York: Columbia University Press, 1944).
[2]Bernard R. Berelson, Paul F. Lazarsfeld, and William N. McPhee, *Voting* (Chicago: University of Chicago Press, 1954).

used in academic polling. This success promoted a national political survey during the 1952 presidential election, which was reported in *The Voter Decides*[3] and which emphasized partisanship, issues, and candidate images. Every two years since 1952 a national election study has been conducted by the Survey Research Center or, more recently, by the Center for Political Studies, a parallel organization within the Institute for Social Research at the University of Michigan. Based mainly on the 1952 and 1956 national surveys, the most impressive study, *The American Voter*,[4] by Campbell, Converse, Miller, and Stokes, continued to emphasize partisanship and political attitudes. Their study is required reading for anyone with a serious interest in American political behavior. Much of the following analysis depends heavily on *The American Voter*, both for substantive findings about the electorate and for analytic organization of the material. *Elections and the Political Order*,[5] also by these authors, covers the 1960 election study as well and pursues the main themes of *The American Voter* in more complex analysis. Analyses of the elections of 1964,[6] 1968,[7] and 1972[8] by the Survey Research Center/Center for Political Studies scholars have appeared in articles in major political science journals and are widely reprinted in collections of readings on political behavior.

The analysis in the following chapters of this book depends heavily on the data from these Survey Research Center and Center for Political Studies national election surveys up to and including the 1984 study. Indeed, a major portion of the research done by American scholars and students of political behavior over the last twenty years has been based upon these data made available through the Inter-

[3]Angus Campbell, Gerald Gurin, and Warren Miller, *The Voter Decides* (Evanston, Ill.: Row, Peterson and Co., 1954).

[4]Angus Campbell et al., *The American Voter* (New York: John Wiley & Sons, 1960).

[5]Angus Campbell et al., *Elections and the Political Order* (New York: John Wiley & Sons, 1966).

[6]Philip E. Converse, Aage R. Clausen, and Warren E. Miller, "Electoral Myth and Reality: The 1964 Election," *American Political Science Review* 59 (June 1965): 321–336.

[7]Philip E. Converse, Warren E. Miller, Jerrold G. Rusk, and Arthur C. Wolfe, "Continuity and Change in American Politics: Parties and Issues in the 1968 Election," *American Political Science Review* 63 (Dec. 1969): 1083–1105.

[8]Arthur H. Miller, Warren E. Miller, Alden S. Raine, and Thad A. Brown, "A Majority Party in Disarray: Policy Polarization in the 1972 Election," *American Political Science Review* 70 (Sept. 1976): 753–778.

university Consortium for Political and Social Research. In 1980, the Center for Political Studies published a large set of data in table form covering the election studies from 1952 to 1978.[9]

Perhaps the great influence of the Survey Research Center and the Center for Political Studies on the study of political behavior is best indicated by their present position as focal point of attack by scholars who argue, from a variety of viewpoints, for a reworking of many of the major conclusions in voting research. On the one hand, some suggest that the findings of *The American Voter* are "time-bound," that is, that they describe the political behavior of Americans only during the relatively placid 1950s and have been inappropriately generalized to other time periods. A more extreme argument suggests that the Survey Research Center analyses underestimated the actual extent of political activity and concern with policy questions among Americans in the 1950s as well as more recently.

An early example of the "revisionist" perspective on voting behavior is V.O. Key's *The Responsible Electorate*,[10] which emphasizes the reasoned nature of attitudes and behavior in the American public. The most extensive study is *The Changing American Voter*[11] by Nie, Verba, and Petrocik, arguing that partisanship has declined and ideological orientation increased among the electorate since the 1950s. Gerald Pomper addresses a variety of similar topics in *Voters' Choice*[12] and Herbert Asher surveys the role of issues in presidential elections since 1952 in *Presidential Elections and American Politics*.[13] A sound collection of readings covering these various views of political behavior is *Controversies in Voting Behavior*[14] edited by Niemi and Weisberg. Another collection of original work, *The Electorate Recon-*

---

[9]Warren E. Miller, Arthur H. Miller, and Edward J. Schneider, *American National Election Studies Data Sourcebook 1952–1978* (Cambridge, Mass.: Harvard University Press, 1980).

[10]V. O. Key, Jr., *The Responsible Electorate* (Cambridge, Mass.: Belknap Press of Harvard University Press, 1966).

[11]Norman H. Nie, Sidney Verba, and John R. Petrocik, *The Changing American Voter* (Cambridge, Mass.: Harvard University Press, 1976).

[12]Gerald Pomper, *Voters' Choice: Varieties of American Electoral Behavior* (New York: Dodd, Mead and Company, 1975).

[13]Herbert Asher, *Presidential Elections and American Politics: Voters, Candidates, and Campaigns since 1952*, 3rd ed. (Homewood, Ill.: The Dorsey Press, 1984).

[14]Richard G. Niemi and Herbert F. Weisberg (eds.), *Controversies in Voting Behavior* (Washington, D.C.: Congressional Quarterly Press, 1984).

sidered[15] edited by John Pierce and John Sullivan, focuses in part on reanalysis of perspectives introduced in *The American Voter*. Several studies of the 1984 election have appeared with *Change and Continuity in the 1984 Elections* by Paul Abramson, John Aldrich and David Rohde being particularly sensitive to theoretical issues.[16]

Several studies of importance deal with selected topics. Paul Abramson in *Generational Change in American Politics*[17] and Philip Converse in *The Dynamics of Party Support*[18] use cohort analysis to examine partisan change over time and arrive at contrary views of the process. The varieties of political participation are examined extensively with a National Opinion Research Center survey by Verba and Nie in *Participation in America*.[19] Two major works on socialization processes are Jennings and Niemi's *The Political Character of Adolescence* and *Generation and Politics*.[20]

Among several formal theoretical works dealing with public opinion and voting, the most prominent is *An Economic Theory of Democracy*,[21] by Anthony Downs; Riker and Ordeshook have surveyed and summarized this field in *An Introduction to Positive Political Theory*[22] and Niemi and Weisberg have collected several of the best papers in this area in *Probability Models of Collective Decision Making*.[23] More and more analysts of electoral behavior have

---

[15]John C. Pierce and John L. Sullivan, *The Electorate Reconsidered* (Beverly Hills, Calif.: Sage Publications, 1980).

[16]Paul R. Abramson, John H. Aldrich, and David W. Rohde, *Change and Continuity in the 1984 Elections* (Washington, D.C.: Congressional Quarterly Press, 1986).

[17]Paul R. Abramson, *Generational Change in American Politics* (Lexington, Mass.: Lexington Books, D. C. Heath and Co., 1975).

[18]Philip E. Converse, *The Dynamics of Party Support: Cohort-Analyzing Party Identification* (Beverly Hills, Calif.: Sage Publications, 1976).

[19]Sidney Verba and Norman H. Nie, *Participation in America: Political Democracy and Social Equality* (New York: Harper & Row, 1972).

[20]M. Kent Jennings and Richard G. Niemi, *The Political Character of Adolescence: The Influence of Families and Schools* (Princeton, N.J.: The Princeton University Press, 1974) and *Generation and Politics* (Princeton, N.J.: Princeton University Press, 1981).

[21]Anthony Downs, *An Economic Theory of Democracy* (New York: Harper & Row, 1957).

[22]William H. Riker and Peter C. Ordeshook, *An Introduction to Positive Political Theory* (Englewood Cliffs, N.J.: Prentice-Hall, 1973).

[23]Richard G. Niemi and Herbert W. Weisberg (eds.), *Probability Models of Collective Decision Making* (Columbus, Ohio: Charles E. Merrill, 1972).

worked within these theoretical frameworks, most notably Benjamin Page[24] and Morris Fiorina.[25]

There are fewer studies of political opinion generally than of voting behavior, although recently John Pierce, Kathleen Beatty, and Paul Hagner have written *The Dynamics of American Public Opinion*, which stresses the role of ideology.[26] In 1978, the American Enterprise Institute began publishing *Public Opinion*, a journal that makes both commentary and data more readily available than heretofore.

Not all of the significant studies of American voting behavior have centered around attitudes or been based on survey data. Much of the work of the late V. O. Key demonstrated how the analysis of election returns could be used to describe and understand political behavior.[27] The Inter-university Consortium for Political and Social Research now offers a practically complete collection of national election returns for major political offices recorded by counties. These data allow more elaborate historical election analysis than has been possible before, and the results of this research are beginning to appear in both history and political science. W. Dean Burnham's *Critical Elections and the Mainsprings of American Politics*[28] and James Sundquist's *Dynamics of the Party System*[29] are both concerned with the occurrence of major realignments in the voting patterns of the electorate, as is *Partisan Realignment* by Clubb, Flanigan, and Zingale.[30] European scholars have done more with aggregate data An excellent collection combining survey data with aggregate data

---

[24]Benjamin Page, *Choices and Echoes in Presidential Elections* (Chicago: University of Chicago Press, 1978).

[25]Morris P. Fiorina, *Retrospective Voting in American National Elections* (New Haven, Conn.: Yale University Press, 1981).

[26]John C. Pierce, Kathleen M. Beatty, and Paul R. Hagner, *The Dynamics of American Public Opinion* (Glenview, Ill.: Scott, Foresman and Co., 1982).

[27]The following articles are good examples of Key's approach: V. O. Key, "A Theory of Critical Elections," *Journal of Politics* 17 (1955): 3–18; and Key and Munger, "Social Determinism and Electoral Decision: The Case of Indiana," *American Voting Behavior*, ed. Eugene Burdick and A. J. Brodbeck (Glencoe, Ill.: Free Press, 1959), pp. 281–299.

[28]Walter Dean Burnham, *Critical Elections and the Mainsprings of American Politics* (New York: W. W. Norton & Co., 1970).

[29]James L. Sundquist, *Dynamics of the Party System*, rev. ed. (Washington, D.C.: The Brookings Institution, 1983).

[30]Jerome M. Clubb, William H. Flanigan, and Nancy H. Zingale, *Partisan Realignment* (Beverly Hills, Calif.: Sage Publications, 1980).

and focusing on European electoral behavior appeared some years ago: Lipset and Rokkan's *Party Systems and Voter Alignments.*[31] Two new cross-national collections based on survey data are: *Electoral Change in Western Democracies,*[32] edited by Crewe and Denver, and *Electoral Change in Advanced Industrial Democracies,*[33] by Dalton, Flanagan, and Beck.

In the past few years many instructional materials in the area of political behavior have become available that allow students to use high-quality data in performing class exercises. The most extensive series of such materials is the SETUPS modules distributed cooperatively by the American Political Science Association and the Interuniversity Consortium for Political and Social Research. Collectively, these modules cover a range of topics in American voting patterns, comparative electoral behavior, and socialization.

---

[31]Seymour M. Lipset and Stein Rokkan, *Party Systems and Voter Alignments: Cross National Perspectives* (New York: The Free Press, 1967).

[32]Ivor Crewe and David Denver (eds.), *Electoral Change in Western Democracies: Patterns and Sources of Electoral Volatility* (London: Croom Helm, 1985).

[33]Russell J. Dalton, Scott C. Flanagan, and Paul Allen Beck (eds.), *Electoral Change in Advanced Industrial Democracies: Realignment or Dealignment?* (Princeton, N.J.: Princeton University Press, 1984).

1

Suffrage
and Turnout

☆☆☆

In 1960, slightly over 60 percent of the eligible electorate voted in the
election for president. By 1984, the turnout of eligible voters had fall-
en to 53 percent. This rather sharp decline in the voting turnout rate
has occasioned a great deal of commentary and more than a little concern about the future of American democracy. The decline in turnout
is viewed as paradoxical because it has occurred at the same time that
the legal impediments to voting have been eliminated or eased and
while the education levels of American citizens are reaching all-time
highs. Americans, with greater opportunities to vote, seem to be
doing so less frequently.

In this chapter, we will put this recent drop in voter turnout into a
broader historical context. We will also look at the factors that make
some individuals more likely to vote than others, and examine how
changes in the political environment can affect whether or not people
vote. In doing so, we will come to some conclusions about what the
decline in turnout does (and does not) mean about the current state of
the democratic process.

1

Extensions of Suffrage

Suffrage, or the *franchise,* means the right to vote. Originally, the U.S. Constitution gave the determination of who should have the right to vote entirely to the states. Later, various amendments were added to the Constitution, restricting the states' abilities to deny the right to vote on the basis of such characteristics as race, sex, or age. However, the basic constitutional provision that gives states the right to set the qualifications for voting remains, and, over the years, states have used such things as the ownership of property, literacy, or length of residency as criteria for granting or withholding the right to vote.

During the colonial period and the early years of the Republic, suffrage was commonly restricted to white males with varying amounts of property; thus, only a small proportion of the adult population was eligible to vote. The severity of the impact of property requirements varied from state to state, and their enforcement varied perhaps even more. Gradually the amount of property held or the amount of taxes paid to obtain suffrage was reduced. Sometimes these changes were hard-won reforms enacted by state legislatures or by state constitutional changes, but in other circumstances practical considerations led to substantial reforms. For example, in the western frontier areas in the nineteenth century, delays in acquiring final title to land holdings made it inexpedient to establish property requirements. Often during the very early years of American history candidates in local elections would simply agree among themselves that all white males could vote rather than try to impose complicated restrictions on the electorate. Only in more settled communities could complex restrictions on suffrage be effectively enforced. On the other hand, in sections of the East, powerful landlords controlled the votes of tenants and often supported their enfranchisement.[1]

After the gradual granting of suffrage to white males, the next major change was the enfranchisement of black males by constitutional amendment in 1870. Even though this change was part of a set of issues so divisive that it had led to civil war, the numerical impact of adding black males was actually rather slight in the nation as a whole. However, unlike other changes in suffrage, this one had a geographical bias: the impact of enfranchising black males was felt almost entirely in the South. (Their subsequent disfranchisement in the South is

---

[1]Chilton Williamson, *American Suffrage from Property to Democracy: 1760–1860* (Princeton, N.J.: Princeton University Press, 1960), especially pp. 131–181.

discussed below.) The next major constitutional extension of voting rights was suffrage for women in 1920. This created by far the most dramatic increase in the proportion of eligible voters, roughly doubling the size of the potential electorate. In the early 1970s, through a combination of federal statutory law and state laws followed by constitutional amendment, the definition of citizenship for purposes of voting was lowered to age eighteen, accomplishing another major extension of the suffrage. These extensions of suffrage, which have not been easy or inevitable, may be explained by the existence of certain political forces. In stable political systems, the extention of suffrage will result from (1) a widely shared commitment to moral principles that entail further grants of suffrage, and (2) the expectation among political leaders that the newly franchised will support the political preferences of the leaders.

The political rhetoric of America carries strong themes of egalitarian democracy. Normally, young people who go through political and civic training in the educational system absorb ideals of individualism and equality. American nationalism, with the myths of the frontier and the melting pot, has justified these values. In part, the goals of American education are participation in and support of American democracy. Although seldom explicitly political in their indoctrination, American religious institutions have reinforced these themes in the political culture, while American literature and theater contribute to political education in these values. The result is that the commitment most Americans have had to equality, individualism, and democracy has provided a basis for supporting extensions of voting rights.

To be sure, there have been counterthemes in American political culture. As in any complex society, conflicting ideals and perspectives contradict and undermine one another. Nevertheless, American political culture has been dominated by ideas and beliefs favoring the extension of voting rights, and when suffrage has been restricted, its restriction has been treated as an exception to more general political principles. Usually a tremendous effort is needed for a subculture to maintain beliefs and values in conflict with the main culture. The "southern system" can be viewed as a subculture of values and social practices partially aimed at keeping blacks from being covered by the general beliefs in equality and individual rights. Although successful for a long time, the imposition of the southern subculture entailed great social and psychological costs.

In the two most dramatic extensions of suffrage, to blacks and to women, political leaders obviously expected the newly enfranchised to support certain policies. Republicans anticipated that black voters in the South after the Civil War would help to secure Republican domination of southern states, and perhaps most southern states passed through a period during which at least some chance existed of combining the votes of blacks and poor whites into a governing majority. The intense prejudice of whites and the difficulty in maintaining the enfranchisement of blacks kept this strategy from working under most circumstances, but a significant element in Republican enthusiasm for black suffrage was the knowledge that Republican voters were being added to the rolls.

Considerable idealism was behind the efforts to enfranchise blacks, and the same idealism appears to have supported suffrage for women. Women were expected to clean up politics once they had the vote; they were seen optimistically as the cure for corruption in government, as unwavering opponents of alcohol, and as champions of virtue in the electorate. Reformers of all sorts hopefully encouraged the enfranchisement of women as a means of promoting their own goals.

No doubt similar factors were at work in the most recent extension of the suffrage to eighteen- to-twenty-year-olds, but perhaps more important was the widespread feeling that a system calling upon young people to fight in the unpopular Vietnam War ought to extend to them the right to participate in the electoral process.

A more unique aspect of the extension of suffrage in the United States is the addition of states in the frontier expansion across the continent. During the decades immediately prior to the Civil War, the politics of slavery dominated political decisions about additions of states, with accompanying expectations as to the policy impact of expansion. Here, too, the question of the expansion of the electorate was dominated largely by concern over the political persuasion of the newly enfranchised voters.

Restrictions on Suffrage

Under the Constitution the states set the qualifications for voters; the three extensions of suffrage by constitutional amendment did not alter this but rather prohibited the states from using certain criteria (race, sex, age) to deny the right to vote. Since states retained the right to impose other restrictions, they have at times used these restrictions to prevent whole classes of people from voting. The most notorious of these efforts was the effective disfranchisement of blacks by the southern states in the late nineteenth and early twentieth centuries.

Several techniques for disfranchising blacks have been used during the past century in the South, and from time to time some of these techniques were applied in the North on a more limited basis to restrict the electoral participation of immigrants. The most common methods included the poll tax, literacy tests, white primaries, discriminatory administrative procedures, and intimidation. The now illegal poll tax, a flat fee charged each individual as a prerequisite for registration to vote, was used for years and no doubt disfranchised both poor blacks and poor whites. In some states, the effect was cumulative, since poll taxes had to be paid for any previous years in which the individual had not voted. The poll tax eventually became less effective, as well as unpopular, with the white voters who had to pay it while the blacks, disfranchised by other means, did not. The literacy test gave local officials a device that could be administered in a selective way to permit registration of whites and practically prohibit the registration of blacks. The "standards of literacy" applied in some cases to blacks precluded registration. To remain effective over long periods of time, these and other similar administrative devices probably depended on the threat or use of violence against blacks. Detailed analysis by Rusk and Stucker[2] of the impact of the poll tax and literacy test from 1876 to 1916 suggests that the poll tax was the more effective device and its efficacy was greatest where the rate was highest and its application most cumulative.

A study of black registration in 1958 by Matthews and Prothro[3] indicated that southern states using poll taxes and literacy tests still inhibited black voter registration after World War II. Matthews and Prothro also demonstrated that the existence of black political and civil rights organizations in a county were associated with increased registration. Surprisingly, incidents of racial violence in the 1950s do not appear to have been associated with black registration. That is,

[2]Jerrold D. Rusk and John J. Stucker, "The Effect of the Southern System of Election Laws on Voting Participation," *The History of American Electoral Behavior*, ed. Joel Silbey, Allan Bogue, and William Flanigan (Princeton, N.J.: Princeton University Press, 1978). See also J. Morgan Kousser, *The Shaping of Southern Politics* (New Haven, Conn.: Yale University Press, 1974), for a treatment of these and many additional topics.

[3]Donald R. Matthews and James W. Prothro, "Political Factors and Negro Voter Registration in the South," *American Political Science Review* 57 (June 1963): 355–367.

6 ✰ CHAPTER 1

high levels of violence did not substantially reduce registration. This does not mean that intimidation was ineffective or that violence served no purpose, but that there was no simple relationship between violence and registration. The poll tax has since been outlawed by amendment to the United States Constitution, and the use of federal voting registrars in the South under the Voting Rights Act of 1965 eliminated the worst excesses in the application of the literacy test. Registration rates in the South for whites and blacks were approximately equal by 1980. Turnout rates in the South have concurrently increased to the point that there is little difference between the North and South in presidential voting.

The outlawing of the poll tax through constitutional amendment and the suspension of literacy tests by the Voting Rights Act of 1965 and its extensions have eliminated two important restrictions on the right to vote.

Other state restrictions on suffrage remain, although of course there is great variation from state to state. In many states, convicted felons cannot vote; in a few, conviction of a felony means the forfeiture of voting rights forever. Residency requirements have been widely used and in the past were often highly restrictive, ranging up to two years of residence in the state required before one was eligible to vote. Highly mobile segments of the population were thus often disfranchised intermittently as each move required a reestablishment of residence. Recently, Supreme Court decisions have limited the permissible residency requirement to fifty days[4] and linked the imposition of a residency requirement to the length of time needed to prepare lists of registered voters before an election.

In the 1980s, the legal barriers to voting have been reduced, for the most part, to the requirement that voters be registered to vote in advance of an election. The inconvenience of administrative arrangements for voter registration and the frequency with which one must re-register offer greater obstacles to voting than do the imposition of other eligibility standards.

The Eligible Electorate

Since throughout American history different state and local election practices have existed, no single set of eligibility requirements can be

---

[4]In 1972, the Court suggested that thirty days was a sufficient length of time to prepare registration lists before an election. Since then they have upheld state laws allowing fifty days.

used as a basis for deciding exactly who belonged to the electorate at any one time. For example, individual states had granted suffrage to blacks, women, and young voters, either in law or in practice, prior to their nationwide enfranchisement. In some states, for many years women were allowed to vote in local and school elections but not in statewide or federal contests. Thus there were many different electorates with different characteristics.

Although extensive data on the characteristics of the national electorate during the first century of the Republic are not available, some reasonable inferences can be drawn from suffrage laws and descriptive data.[5] The voters of 1789 can be described as white male adults who held some property. In the most permissive states, 80 percent or more of the white male adults may have been eligible to vote; in the most restrictive states, less than 10 percent were eligible to vote. By 1850, property qualifications still existed in some states, but in many areas restrictions on white males had all but disappeared.

Of course, during the early years of the Republic, almost all voters resided in rural areas. The electorate has become steadily more urban since then, becoming predominantly city and town dwellers by the mid-twentieth century. The literacy rate of the electorate was high from the beginning, although the level of education was not. During the nineteenth century only a very small fraction of Americans (about 2 or 3 percent) graduated from high school, but the rate increased rapidly during the first half of the twentieth century to the point where now every year about two-thirds of the seventeen-year-olds graduate from high school. When blacks were enfranchised after the Civil War, the overwhelming majority were illiterate, even though only about half of them had recently been slaves. The illiteracy rate among blacks has steadily declined and presently approaches the very low rate among whites.

After Reconstruction, blacks were disenfranchised in state after state in the South, regardless of their literacy. By the early part of the twentieth century, some blacks enjoyed the vote in certain areas, and women had acquired the vote in various types of elections. White males, however, formed the bulk of the electorate. During this period, large numbers of immigrants joined the electorate. Additional data probably would show that the number of naturalized citizens in the electorate never exceeded 25 percent, and now represents a

---

[5]U.S. Bureau of the Census, *Historical Statistics of the United States, Colonial Times to 1957; Continuation to 1962 and Revisions* (Washington, D.C.: U.S. Government Printing Office, 1965), p. 207, p. 65, p. 9.

decreasing proportion of it. Despite the unfair social and economic aspects of the reception and treatment of immigrants, the political system accommodated millions of people from abroad without great stress.

After 1920, women were added to the electorate, and in the North the eligible electorate and the adult population were roughly equivalent. As late as 1950, large numbers of southern blacks were still effectively excluded from the electorate, but this has changed steadily since the early 1960s. After 1971, the addition of younger voters changed the eligible electorate once again.

Turnout in American Elections

Surely one of the most persistent complaints about the American electoral system in the twentieth century is its failure to achieve the high rates of voter turnout found in other countries and common in this country in the nineteenth century. Figure 1–1 shows voting turnout in the United States was close to 80 percent prior to 1900; modern democracies around the world frequently record similarly high levels. Turnout in the United States during the twentieth century, in contrast, has exceeded 60 percent only in presidential elections, and in recent years the figure has been closer to 50 percent. These unfavorable comparisons are misleading on several grounds. The *voting turnout rate* is the percentage of the eligible population that actually votes in a particular election. In the United States, this is usually calculated as the number of votes cast divided by the total number of eligible adult citizens. The definition of "eligible adult" takes into account the historical changes in eligibility occasioned by the extension of suffrage to blacks, women, and eighteen-year-olds, but it does not take into account state restrictions on eligibility, such as registration requirements. As we have seen, these restrictions may be substantial. Thus some of those included in the "eligible population" are not really able to vote, and the turnout rate, calculated in this way, appears lower than it actually is. (And, in some states historically, blacks, women, and eighteen-year-olds were given the right to vote before suffrage was extended to them by amendment to the national Constitution; not including them in the denominator makes the turnout rate appear higher than it really was.)

In most foreign countries, the rate of turnout is based on lists of registered voters rather than on the total eligible electorate or the adult population. There are no detailed comparative studies of

FIGURE 1–1 Estimated Turnout of Eligible Voters in Presidential Elections in the South and Non-South, 1860–1984

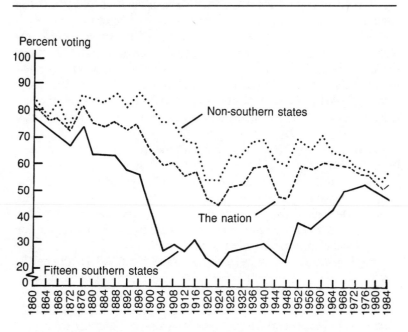

Sources: Robert Lane, *Political Life* (New York: The Free Press of Glencoe, 1959), p. 20; U.S. Bureau of the Census, *Statistical Abstract of the United States: 1986,* 106th ed. (Washington, D.C.: U.S. Government Printing Office, 1985), p. 517; Walter Dean Burnham, ''The Changing Shape of the American Political Universe,'' *American Political Science Review* 59 (March 1955): 11, Figure 1.

voting, but the reported rates in other countries may exaggerate turnout by 15 percent or more in comparison with the United States. The most careful estimate of American turnout takes into account all the various restrictions and concludes that turnout in the 1960 presidential election was more than 80 percent of the eligible electorate.[6] This rate is about 20 percent higher than the "official" rate in Figure 1–1. To facilitate comparison with other years, the lower rates will be used in the following discussion, but we need to bear these factors in mind

---

[6]William G. Andrews, "American Voting Participation," *The Western Political Quarterly* 19 (1966): 639.

as we consider the ups and downs in voter turnout recently and over the past 200 years.

Looking again at Figure 1-1, it is apparent that some dramatic changes have occurred historically in the rate of voter turnout. Each major extension of suffrage—in 1868, in 1920, and in 1971—was marked by a drop in the proportion of the electorate voting. Perhaps this is not surprising, since the newly eligible voters might be expected to take some time to acquire the habit of exercising their right to vote. It should also be noted that the drop in the turnout rate occasioned by the extension of the suffrage was, in each case, the continuation of a downward trend.

During the nineteenth century, national turnout appears to have been extremely high—always over 70 percent. The decline in national turnout from shortly before 1900 to 1916 is in part attributable to the restriction of black voting in the South. This decline in voting in the South also resulted from the increasing one-party domination of the region, since a far lower turnout existed than can be accounted for simply by the disfranchisement of blacks.

Explaining the voting record shown in Figure 1-1 for the northern states presents a more difficult problem, since there was a substantial decline in turnout in the first two decades of the twentieth century and turnout has never returned to its previous levels. The disfranchisement of blacks and whites in the South cannot account for northern nonvoting.

There are two quite different explanations of the decline in voting in the North that commenced in the late 1890s. A persuasive case has been made by Schattschneider[7] and Burnham[8] in their studies of this period. Basically, they contend that a high level of party loyalty and political involvement during the last quarter of the nineteenth century caused high turnout and great partisan stability. Then during the 1890s, electoral patterns shifted in such a way that the South became safely Democratic, and most of the rest of the nation came under the domination of the Republican party. Schattschneider's analysis emphasizes the extent to which this alignment enabled conservatives in both regions to dominate American politics for many years. According to this line of argument, one consequence of declining competition and greater conservatism throughout the electoral system was a loss of

[7]E. E. Schattschneider, *The Semisovereign People* (New York: Holt, Rinehart and Winston, 1960), especially chapter 5.

[8]Walter Dean Burnham, "The Changing Shape of the American Political Universe," *American Political Science Review* 59 (March 1965): 7–28.

interest in politics accompanied by lower turnout and less partisan loyalty in the early twentieth century. Burnham emphasizes the disintegration of party voting with more ticket splitting and lower turnout in off-year elections.

Some elements of this account are undeniably accurate. Electoral patterns did change somewhat around the turn of the century, with many regions of the nation changing from competitive to one-party areas. Throughout areas previously characterized by high turnout, straight ticket voting, and stable voting patterns, turnout and partisan stability suffered greater fluctuations.

An alternative set of arguments is consistent with these patterns but gives them a different interpretation.[9] The high rate of turnout in the nineteenth century may not have resulted from political involvement by an interested, well-informed electorate, but on the contrary it may have been possible at all only because of low levels of information and interest. During the last half of the nineteenth century, a largely uninformed electorate was aroused to vote by means of extreme and emotional political appeals. Presumably, in the absence of more general awareness of the political situation, these alarmist arguments produced firm commitments to vote. But by and large, the parties manipulated the electorate—a manipulation possible because the electorate was not well informed.

Furthermore, this argument alleges that the party organizations "delivered" or "voted" substantial numbers of voters during this period. Thus, the remarkable stability of party voting may be a testimony to the corruption of the party organizations. The decline of stable party voting in the early twentieth century coincides with various attacks on political corruption and party machines. The resultant weakening of party machines and increased honesty in electoral activities could have reduced turnout. In fact, the apparent hostility of the electorate to the parties throughout this period seems inconsistent with strong party loyalty. A study by Jerrold Rusk[10] shows dramatic

---

[9]The most general statement of this argument is found in Philip E. Converse, "Change in the American Electorate," *The Human Meaning of Social Change*, ed. Angus Campbell and Philip E. Converse (New York: Russell Sage Foundation, 1972), pp. 263–337. For an analysis that alters the estimates of turnout, see Ray M. Shortridge, "Estimating Voter Participation," *Analyzing Electoral History*, ed. Jerome M. Clubb, William H. Flanigan, and Nancy H. Zingale (Beverly Hills, Calif.: Sage Publications, 1981), pp. 137–152.

[10]Jerrold D. Rusk, "The Effect of the Australian Ballot Reform on Split Ticket Voting: 1876–1908," *American Political Science Review* 64 (December 1970): 1220–1238.

changes in voting patterns associated with electoral reform laws, especially the introduction of the Australian ballot. Prior to the introduction of electoral reforms, voting was often not secret; distinctively colored ballots prepared by the political parties and limited to one party were distributed to voters, marked, and openly placed in the ballot box.

Another of the reforms instituted during the early twentieth century to combat corruption was the imposition of a system of voter registration. Besides limiting the opportunities for fraudulent voting, registration requirements created an additional barrier to the act of voting that had the effect of causing the least motivated potential voters to drop out of the electorate. Many states introduced permanent or semi-permanent forms of registration; however, in others, like New York, where annual registration was required in many cities, the barrier to voting could be formidable. The impact of registration is heavy on the mobile segments of the population because each move requires registering anew. In the 1970s, the Middle Atlantic states, with their mobile populations and traditionally rigorous registration requirements, had as high a rate of unregistered citizens as did the states of the Confederacy with their legacy of racial discrimination. In an extensive study of turnout, Wolfinger and Rosenstone estimated that easing the procedures for registration would increase turnout by 9 percent.[11] Since most nonvoters are not registered—the best estimates show three out of four nonvoters are not registered—in order for turnout to increase substantially there must be increased voter registration.[12] Some states have moved toward "same-day" registration in efforts to remove impediments to voting and increase electoral turnout. Even so, registration and associated residency requirements remain the most important legal restriction on voting today.

After reaching an all-time low in the early 1920s, turnout in national elections increased steadily until 1940. There was a substantial drop in turnout during World War II and immediately thereafter, and since 1960 there has been a gradual decline. Great differences in turnout among the states are concealed within these national data. As Figure 1-1 shows, rates of voting in the South were consistently low until recently when they nearly converge with northern turnout. Re-

---

[11]Raymond E. Wolfinger and Steven J. Rosenstone, *Who Votes?* (New Haven, Conn.: Yale University Press, 1980), p. 73.

[12]These estimates may exaggerate nonregistration because some nonvoters may rationalize their failure to vote on technical grounds. For example, some nonvoters give this reason where there are no registration requirements.

gional differences in turnout in presidential voting have almost disappeared; state variation within regions, however, is still considerable.

"High-Stimulus" and "Low-Stimulus" Elections

Elections vary in the amount of interest and attention they generate in the electorate. As can be seen in Figure 1–2, presidential elections draw high turnout, whereas off-year congressional elections are characterized by lower levels of turnout. Even in a presidential election year, fewer people vote in congressional elections than vote for president, but the dramatic decline in turnout is the 10 to 20 percent decline in voting in off-year elections. Primaries and local elections elicit still lower turnout. At least some of these differences can be accounted for by the lower visibility of these latter elections, making a lesser amount of information about them available to the voter and producing a lower level of interest in them. Differences in the level of turnout for any given type of election can also be expected to vary with the amount of interest in that particular race.

A number of elements would seem to influence the amount of interest in an election. The differences in level of interest from presidential elections to congressional elections to local elections can be viewed as a result of these factors:

1. Differences in media coverage given the election
2. Significance attached by voters to the office
3. Importance of issues raised in the campaign
4. Attractiveness of candidates

Variation in these factors leads to what Angus Campbell called "high-stimulus" and "low-stimulus" elections.[13]

Newspapers and television give far more coverage to the activities and speeches of presidential candidates than to those of congressional candidates. Even the most indifferent citizen comes to possess impressions and some information about presidential candidates and their campaigns. Bombardment through the mass media awakens the rela-

---

[13]Angus Campbell et al., *Elections and the Political Order* (New York: John Wiley & Sons, 1966), pp. 40–62.

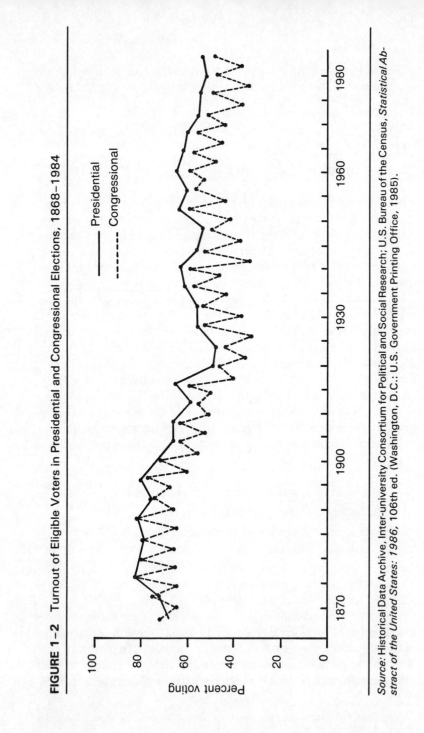

FIGURE 1-2 Turnout of Eligible Voters in Presidential and Congressional Elections, 1868–1984

Presidential
Congressional

Percent voting

1870 1900 1930 1960 1980

Source: Historical Data Archive, Inter-university Consortium for Political and Social Research; U.S. Bureau of the Census, *Statistical Abstract of the United States: 1986,* 106th ed. (Washington, D.C.: U.S. Government Printing Office, 1985).

tively uninterested and often provides them with some reason for bothering to vote. This is not nearly so likely to happen in other election campaigns, where only the motivated citizens will become informed and concerned to any degree. Even so, a week or so after the election, a substantial proportion of the voters will not recall the name of the congressional candidate for whom they voted.

The factors of media coverage, the significance of the office, and the importance of the issues do a better job of explaining the difference in the levels of turnout in presidential elections versus other kinds of elections than they do among presidential elections themselves. None of these factors can account for the decline in turnout in presidential voting over the last two decades. Media coverage and campaigning through the media have increased; there is no evidence that the significance attached to the presidency has declined; and critical issues have been intensely debated, such as civil rights and the Vietnam War in 1968, the War again in 1972, and the Iranian hostage crisis and inflation in 1980. Yet a steady erosion in turnout occurred through these years. The lack of attractiveness of the presidential candidates has often been cited as a possible explanation, contrasting the enormously popular Eisenhower in 1952 and 1956 with the "lesser of two evils" contests of the late 1960s and 1970s. But even in the election of 1984, featuring an incumbent president who had gained tremendous personal popularity, voter turnout remained at a low ebb.

Another factor often thought to raise the level of turnout in an election, perhaps by increasing the level of interest, is the degree of competition between the parties. Presumably, the closer and more uncertain the outcome, the more people will see their vote as potentially decisive. Undeniably, the virtual absence of party competition in the South during the period of black disfranchisement was associated with extremely low levels of turnout, even among white voters. And both turnout and competition in the South have increased since blacks have joined the electorate. On the other hand, the elections of 1968, 1976, and 1980 suggest that the expectation of a close race does not invariably lead to heightened turnout nor, as 1984 shows, does the expectation of a landslide depress turnout.

Another form of competitiveness probably has more relationship to the level of turnout. The decision to allow a race to remain uncontested or to offer only a "sacrificial lamb" can dramatically reduce turnout. In contrast, a hotly contested race with strenuous activity by party organizations is likely to get more voters to the polls on election day, even though the final outcome may not be particularly close. Recently, public financing of presidential campaigns and of some state election campaigns has been undertaken with concomitant legal limitations on campaign spending. It is not clear to what degree, if any, campaign financing laws have reduced or equalized the level of party organizational activity. The limitations on spending in presidential campaigns since 1976 do seem to have forced an organizational separation between the national campaign and local party efforts. Variations in turnout may therefore be more the result of local campaign efforts than of national factors. To measure the degree of partisan campaign activity across the nation would be extremely difficult, but common sense and the folklore of campaign strategy suggest that the greater the amount of effort exerted, the higher the level of turnout.

Voters and Nonvoters

All but a small proportion of the population votes at least occasionally, but individuals vary in the regularity with which they cast their ballots. Certainly, individual interest in politics is one factor creating such differences. And, as one would expect, the probability of voting increases at each level of expressed interest in political campaigns. In the last section, the level of interest in a campaign was treated as a characteristic of the political environment, generated by the importance of the office at stake, the amount of media coverage, and so on. But interest and involvement in politics are also individual characteristics and individuals vary substantially in the attention they pay to politics, their involvement in politics, and the amount of information about candidates and issues they acquire. As one would expect, the probability of voting increases at each level of expressed interest and involvement in political campaigns. Figure 1-3 illustrates this relationship: the highly interested, informed, and concerned citizens (a combination of characteristics highly valued in the belief system of a democratic society) turn out to cast their ballots on election day, whereas the apathetic, ill-informed and uninterested stay at home. Figure 1-3 also draws attention to two "deviant cases" that run contrary to the expected pattern.

The first deviant condition, "alienation," is characterized by high interest and low turnout. The situation may be one of voluntary alienation in which individuals withdraw from political participation purposefully. Their high level of interest and information implies some reason for their withdrawal; they are dissatisfied with, or offended by, the political system. "Nonvoluntary alienation" refers to situa-

FIGURE 1-3 Relationship between Electoral Turnout and Interest, Involvement, and Information

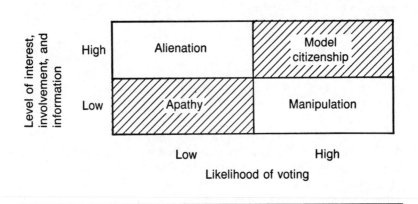

Level of interest, involvement, and information

Likelihood of voting

tions in which interested potential voters are prevented from participating. Both situations are dangerous to the political system because highly interested and informed citizens who do not participate have the potential for extremely disruptive activities. So far as we know, alienation in this form is uncommon in American politics. In each presidential election since 1968 there has been speculation that large numbers of potential voters were dissatisfied with the candidates and would not case a ballot for president. Even though the elections from 1968 to 1984 drew lower turnouts than 1964 or 1960, there is no reason to believe that a sizable proportion of the nonvoters were positively alienated. When nonvoters were asked in 1968 why they did not vote, only about 3 percent specifically mentioned unhappiness with the available choices. Similarly, a study focusing primarily on the causes of nonvoting in the 1976 election found voters and nonvoters to be quite similar in their levels of alienation and cynicism toward politics; for only 6 percent of the nonvoters was rejection of politics the main explanation of their nonvoting.[14]

The second deviant case, "manipulation," describes voters characterized by low interest and high turnout. It refers to a situation in which individuals with little information or interest become involved in voting. Presumably, this "manipulation" is achieved by getting individuals to vote either through coercion or by highly stimu-

[14]Arthur T. Hadley, *The Empty Polling Booth* (Englewood Cliffs, N.J.: Prentice-Hall, 1978), pp. 20, 41.

lating and arousing appeals. Coercive methods for assuring turnout
may range from police-state orders to fines for failure to vote. More
common in the American political system are exceptionally moving or
alarming appeals, bringing to the polls people so unsophisticated that
they are easily moved. Very high levels of turnout can be inspired by
emotional, inflammatory appeals; indeed, this is one possible explanation for the high turnout levels in the United States for many years
after the Civil War. Campaigns were marked by extreme appeals,
and, since education levels were low, it is reasonable to suspect that
there were lower levels of interest and information than during the
twentieth century.

Even though interest in politics is strongly correlated with voting,
about half of those who say they have "not much" interest do in fact
vote in presidential elections, suggesting that still other factors are also
at work. One of these is a sense of civic duty—the attitude that a good
citizen has an obligation to vote, that it is important to vote, regardless of the expected impact on the outcome. Since such feelings are
usually a prime focus of the political socialization carried on in the
American educational system, turnout is highest among those with
the longest exposure to this system: Length of education is one of the
best predictors of an individual's likelihood of voting.

Because education is so closely associated with relative affluence
and social status, people who vote are usually slightly better off in socioeconomic terms than the population as a whole. This bias is likely
to increase in low-stimulus elections, as greater numbers of occasional
voters drop out of the electorate, leaving the field to the better
educated and more affluent who rarely miss an election. Austin
Ranney,[15] in studying the 1968 presidential primaries in New
Hampshire and Wisconsin, has shown that voters were better off and
more intense in their issue preferences than nonvoters.

Another important factor contributing to nonvoting is age; a relatively large proportion of young people pass up their first opportunities to vote. This situation has been magnified in presidential elections
in the 1970s. The extension of the franchise to eighteen-year-olds
enlarged the pool of eligible young voters, and turnout has dropped to
its lowest point since 1948. Table 1–1 shows the likelihood of voting
increasing from young adulthood through middle age, with a subsequent downturn among the aged.

---

[15]Austin Ranney, "Turnout and Representation in Presidential Primary Elections," *American Political Science Review* 66 (March 1972): 21–37.

TABLE 1-1 Percentage of the Electorate Reporting Having Voted in the Presidential Election of 1984 by Age

18-21	22-24	25-34	35-44	45-54	55-64	65-74	75 and over
45%	55%	70%	79%	81%	83%	84%	68%

Source: Center for Political Studies 1984 National Election Study.

Much of the nonvoting among young people may be attributed to the unsettled circumstances of this age group rather than to simple disinterest in politics, although young people are slightly less interested than older people of similar educational levels. Military service, geographic mobility with the possible failure to meet residence requirements, the additional hurdle of initial registration—all create barriers to voting for the young that are less likely to affect older voters. The tendency of young people not to vote is partially offset by their generally higher levels of education. As Figure 1-4 shows, while the turnout of middle-aged people is higher at each educational level than that of young adults, the gap narrows among the college educated.

If only registered voters are considered, a different pattern emerges. Turnout is generally very high, and the relationships between turnout and either age or education are much weaker. Among those registered to vote, the difference in turnout between the grade-school educated and the college educated is only 10 percent. Age-related differences in turnout among the registered are also small. There is a tendency for these nonvoters to be less interested in politics than voters, but their interest is much higher than for the unregistered.

A little less than half of the members of the electorate who were not registered in 1980 had registered and voted in previous elections. These individuals have had their registration interrupted, perhaps by changing their residence, and probably will return to the active electorate. Presumably there is a steady movement of some members of the electorate into and out of registration, but only a very small proportion remain completely outside the active electorate permanently.

By age thirty-five, most people have joined the voting population at least on an occasional basis. A small proportion of the middle-aged and older group remains outside the voting public. These habitual nonvoters, who have passed up several opportunities to vote, are less than 5 percent of the total electorate, according to current survey re-

FIGURE 1–4 Turnout in the 1984 Presidential Election According to Age and Education

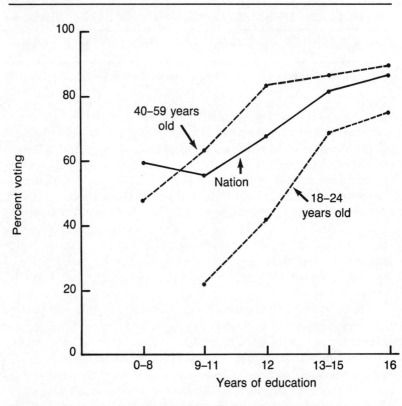

40–59 years old

Nation

18–24 years old

Percent voting

Years of education

0–8   9–11   12   13–15   16

Source: Center for Political Studies 1984 National Election Study.

search estimates.[16] This group has been steadily decreasing in size, and presumably the social forces that brought about this decrease will reduce it still further. In the past, this group of habital nonvoters has been disproportionately southern, black, and female. Restrictions against black suffrage, coupled with a traditional culture that worked against active participation of women in civic life, meant that as

[16]This "best estimate" of individuals outside the political system is unquestionably low. First, a disproportionately large number of people outside the political system would not even be included in the population of households from which the sample is drawn. Second, many of those in the sample who were never contacted or who refused to be interviewed would probably be classified as outside the political system.

recently as 1952 in the South, large proportions of blacks of both sexes, as well as white women, had never voted in a presidential election. Figure 1–5, which includes all respondents who have never voted, shows that dramatic changes have taken place in southern voting patterns in the last three decades. At the same time, the somewhat lower educational and income levels in the South have meant that southern-

FIGURE 1–5 The Percentage of Adults Who Have Never Voted, According to Race and Sex for the South and Non-South, 1952–1980

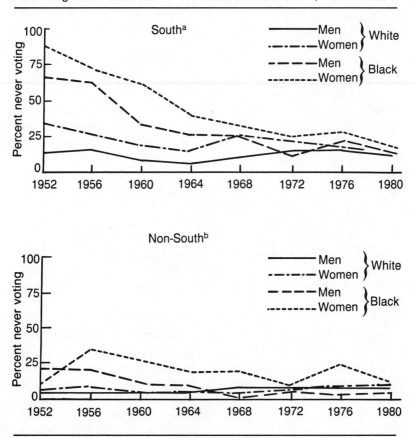

[a]The states included in the South are Alabama, Arkansas, Florida, Georgia, Kentucky, Louisiana, Maryland, Mississippi, North Carolina, Oklahoma, South Carolina, Tennessee, Texas, Virginia, and West Virginia.
[b]The states included in the non-South are the remainder.

Source: Survey Research Center/Center for Political Studies National Election Studies.

ers have been, and still are, somewhat more likely to remain outside the electorate than their counterparts in the North. (In Figure 1–5, the relatively large proportion of northern black women who in 1976 report never having voted is entirely attributable to young women who have only passed up one or two opportunities to vote.) Habitual nonvoters over age thirty-five are still disproportionately southern and female, but they now include only slightly more blacks than the rest of the population. On the other hand, over half of these people have only grade-school educations, and one-third are over sixty-five years old, suggesting that mass education, changing mores about political activity for women, and continued facilitation of black suffrage in the future will bring all but a tiny portion of the population into the arena of political participation.

We need to return to the question of accounting for the decline in turnout over the last two decades. As we have seen, legal restrictions on voting have eased and education levels have increased; these circumstances should be expected to increase turnout, yet they have apparently been more than offset by other factors. One suggestion has focused on the expansion of the electorate in 1971 to include eighteen-year-olds. Since young people are less likely to vote than older people, their inclusion in the electorate would be expected to decrease turnout, other things being equal. Apparently, however, this can account for only a small portion of the decline.

Another possibility, raised by political commentators in 1972, 1980, and 1984, is that "calling the election" early in the evening, before the polls close in some parts of the country, reduces turnout. Once potential voters learn that a television network has declared a winner in the race for president, the argument goes, they will no longer be interested in voting for president or any other office. The potential impact would have been even greater in 1980 when President Carter conceded to Reagan before the polls closed in the West. On the other hand, the 1976 election was so close that the winner was not known until the wee hours of the following day (when the polls had closed in all fifty states) and there was no appreciable impact on turnout. The evidence on this matter is inconclusive but there is no clear demonstration that these factors have influenced turnout in a significant way.[17]

---

[17]See Laurily K. Epstein and Gerald Strom, "Election Night Projections and West Coast Turnout," *American Politics Quarterly* 9 (October 1981): 479–491, and Raymond Wolfinger and Peter Linquiti, "Tuning In and Turning Out," *Public Opinion* (February–March 1981).

A somewhat more sweeping form of this argument—and one harder to test—suggests that the style of media coverage of the campaign has turned elections into a "spectator sport" which voters watch with varying degrees of interest but feel no need for involvement. The prediction of the winner in polls, the focus in presidential debates on who won rather than on substance, the attention to the "horse race" aspects of the primary campaigns, and the networks' race to call the election first are all alleged to be factors in this withdrawal of the voter from active participation.

The most careful assessment of the reasons for the decline in voter turnout has been done by Paul Abramson and John Aldrich.[18] Analyzing survey responses in all presidential and congressional elections from 1952 to 1980, they conclude that approximately two-thirds of the decline in turnout over this time period can be attributed to two factors: a decline in the perceptions of voters that government is responsive to them and their needs; and a decline in the partisanship of voters. Clearly, if voters increasingly feel that government is unlikely to listen to their preferences, there is less incentive to express those preferences through voting. Similarly, as we shall see in the next chapter, having a preference for one party over the other usually involves seeing some important differences between the parties and a concern over which party takes control of government. Failure to see much difference between the parties leads to nonparticipation in the choice between the candidates representing those parties.

Throughout this discussion of turnout, we have implied the need for an explanation of nonvoting; we have assumed voting is "normal" or to be expected. However, this topic could be approached quite differently. The question could be asked, "Why do people bother to vote?" as if nonvoting were the natural pattern or expected behavior and voting required explanation. The answer that one vote can determine the outcome of an election and that most people vote anticipating that their vote may be crucial defies reason as well as some evidence. One vote rarely decides an election, although many races are close, and no reasonable voter should expect to cast the deciding vote in an election.

There is, however, another sense in which "votes count" in an election, and that is as an expression of preference for a candidate or for a party, regardless of whether that candidate ultimately wins or

---

[18]Paul R. Abramson and John H. Aldrich, "The Decline of Electoral Participation in America," *American Political Science Review* 76 (September 1982): 502–521.

loses. Elections are more than simply a mechanism for selecting public officials; they are also a means for communicating, albeit somewhat dimly, a set of attitudes to government. For most Americans, voting remains the only means of influence regularly employed. Many see it as the only avenue open to ordinary citizens to make government listen to their needs. The desire to be counted on one side of the fence or the other and the feeling that one ought to be so counted are perhaps the greatest spurs to voting. The recent decline in turnout suggests that fewer Americans are responding to these feelings.

2

Partisanship

One of the most frequently debated questions in contemporary political commentary is the extent to which the victories of Ronald Reagan at the polls in 1980 and 1984 have been the occasion for a fundamental restructuring—or realignment—of the partisan divisions in the American public. A second question is whether political parties in the United States have lost their capacity to attract and retain the loyalty of the American voter. Both these questions bear on the issue of *partisanship*—the sense of attachment or belonging that an individual feels for a political party. In this and the next two chapters we will explore the concept of partisanship and its implications for political behavior. In this chapter, we will discuss the meaning of partisanship, its measurement, and the effect that having or not having partisanship has on the way people act politically. In Chapter 3, we will examine the social characteristics of partisans and independents. In Chapter 4, we will consider how partisanship changes over the lifetime of the individual, between generations and over the course of American political history.

Party Loyalty

For more than one hundred years, the United States electorate has supported a two-party system in national politics, which is a remarkable stability unknown in other democracies. Within this stable party system, however, voter support for Republicans and Democrats has fluctuated widely, and voters occasionally abandon the traditional parties altogether to support third-party or independent candidates. The aggregate vote totals for presidential elections, shown in Figure 2–1, reveal a wide range of party fortunes, even in elections close together in time. The Democratic vote, for example, swings from a low of 42 percent for Stevenson in his 1956 try against Eisenhower to a high of 61 percent for Johnson against Goldwater in 1964. Eight years later in 1972, the Democrats hit another low with McGovern winning just 37 percent of the vote against the incumbent President Nixon.

These recent elections are not unusual in this respect. The history of presidential voting, shown from 1824 to 1984 in Figure 2–1, shows a generally erratic pattern with only one series of very close elections in the last quarter of the nineteenth century. Some of the more dramatic fluctuations have involved the appearance of strong third-party candidates. In 1912, for example, Theodore Roosevelt cut so heavily into Republican party support that a party with an overwhelming advantage lost the election. In 1968, more than 13 percent of the voters, mainly but not exclusively in the South, deserted the two main parties to vote for George Wallace. Most recently, John Anderson's independent candidacy won 7 percent of the vote in 1980.

Despite these variations in election outcomes and despite the demonstrated capacity of American voters for highly selective and differentiated support for candidates offered them by the political parties, most voters have a basic and quite stable loyalty to one party or the other. This underlying party loyalty is of interest to political analysts partially because it provides a base against which to measure deviations in particular elections. In other words, the individual voter's long-standing loyalty to one party means that, "other things being equal," or in the absence of disrupting forces, he or she can be expected to vote for that party. However, voters are responsive to a great variety of other influences that can either strengthen or weaken their tendency to vote for their usual party. Obvious variations occur from election to election in the attractiveness of the candidates, the impact of foreign and domestic policy issues, and purely local circumstances. These current factors, often called "short-term forces," may move voters away from their normal party choices.[1] The concept of

---

[1]For the most important statement of these ideas, see Philip E. Converse, "The Concept of a Normal Vote," *Elections and the Political Order*, ed. Angus Campbell et al. (New York: John Wiley & Sons, 1966), pp. 9–39.

FIGURE 2–1 Partisan Division of the Presidential Vote in the Nation, 1824–1984

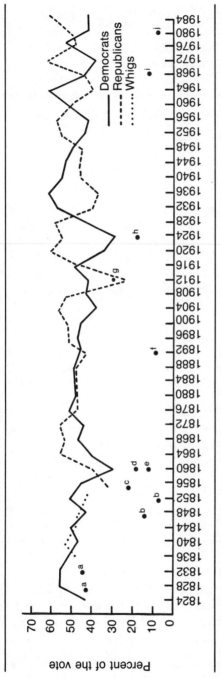

Other parties gaining at least 5% of the vote: [a]National Republican; [b]Free Soil; [c]American; [d]Southern Democratic; [e]Constitutional Union; [f]People's; [g]Bull Moose; [h]Progressive; [i]American Independent; [j]Anderson Independent Candidacy

Note: While presenting these data, we have not bothered to draw attention to the wide range of errors that may exist. There are errors in collecting and recording data as well as errors in computation. The presidential election of 1960 provides an illustration of another form of uncertainty that enters into these data — choices made among alternative ways of presenting the data. It is customary to list the popular vote in such a way that Kennedy appears a narrow winner over Nixon in 1960. Actually in order to reach this distribution of the total vote, it is necessary to exaggerate the Kennedy vote from Alabama, since on the slate of Democratic electors in Alabama there were uncommitted electors. Eventually six of the uncommitted electors voted for Harry Byrd; five electors voted for Kennedy. If the Kennedy popular vote in Alabama is reduced to a proportion, say 5/11 in this case, of the vote for Democratic electors and if only this reduced popular vote is added to his national total, Nixon, not Kennedy, has the larger popular vote total nationally in 1960. In percentages these are negligible changes, but symbolically such differences can become important. In these tables we have followed the usual practice of presenting the augmented Kennedy total.

Source: Historical Data Archive, Inter-university Consortium for Political and Social Research.

party loyalty can thus be used as a base of comparison against which to measure departures in the actual vote of the electorate.

The tendency of most individuals to be basically loyal to one political party or another also makes the idea of partisanship one of the most useful concepts for understanding the political behavior of individuals. The availability of good survey data in recent decades makes it possible to assess individual partisanship, or party identification, and to relate this to other aspects of political behavior.

Party Identification

The pioneer studies in voting behavior ignored partisanship, emphasizing instead social variables like religion and occupation. Since the first major study by Angus Campbell and his colleagues at the Survey Research Center in 1952,[2] party identification has assumed a central role in all voting behavior analysis. Party identification is a relatively uncomplicated measure determined by responses to the following questions:

> *"Generally speaking, do you usually think of yourself as a Republican, a Democrat, an independent, or what? Would you call yourself a strong (R), (D) or a not very strong (R), (D)? (If "independent") Do you think of yourself as closer to the Republican party or to the Democratic party?"*

Leaving aside for the moment the people who do not or cannot respond to such a question, we have seven categories of more-or-less active participants in the electorate according to intensity of partisanship:

Strong Democrats	Weak Democrats	Independent Democrats	Independents	Independent Republicans	Weak Republicans	Strong Republicans

———————————————————— 0 ————————————————————
Partisanship

As this self-identification measure of party loyalty is the best indicator of partisanship, political analysts commonly refer to partisanship and party identification interchangeably. Partisanship is the sin-

---

[2]Angus Campbell, Gerald Gurin, and Warren Miller, *The Voter Decides* (Evanston, Ill.: Row, Peterson and Co., 1954).

gle most important influence on political opinions and voting behavior. Many other influences are at work on voters in our society, and partisanship varies in its importance in different types of elections and in different time periods; nevertheless, no other single factor compares in significance with partisanship.[3]

Partisanship represents the feeling of sympathy for and loyalty to a political party that an individual acquires (probably) during childhood and holds (usually) with increasing intensity throughout life. Since most individuals think of themselves as something politically, this self-image as a Democrat or a Republican is useful to the individual in a special way. For example, individuals who think of themselves as Republicans respond to political information partially by using party identification to orient themselves, reacting to new information in such a way that it fits in with the ideals and feelings they already have. A Republican who hears a Republican party leader advocate a policy has a basis in party loyalty for supporting the policy, quite apart from other considerations. Or a Democrat may feel favorably inclined toward a candidate for office because that candidate bears the Democratic label. Partisanship may orient individuals in their political environment, but it may also distort their picture of reality.

As can be seen in Table 2–1, the distribution of partisans has been quite stable over the past forty years, although some significant changes are becoming apparent in the most recent period. During these years, the Democrats have held a substantial advantage over the Republicans, an advantage ranging from three to two in 1956 to a high of two to one in 1964. This means, among other things, that in the nation as a whole the Democratic party has begun campaigns with many more supporters than has the Republican party. Broadly speaking, the Democrats have tried to hold onto their following during a campaign, while the Republicans have had to attempt to win over a following.

For many years the advantage that the Democrats enjoyed nationally was largely a result of the overwhelming majority of Democrats in the South, as shown in Table 2–2. Today, Democrats are still stronger in the South than in the North, though the proportion of Republicans in the South has increased to about the same level as in the

---

[3]The most important work on party identification is in Angus Campbell et al., *The American Voter* (New York: John Wiley & Sons, 1960), pp. 120–167. For a more recent treatment in comparative perspective, see Ian Budge, Ivor Crewe, and Dennis Farlie (eds.), *Party Identification and Beyond* (New York: John Wiley & Sons, 1976), Part I.

TABLE 2–1 The Party Identification of the Electorate, 1940–1984

	1940	1944	1947	1952	1954	1956	1958	1960	1962	1964	1966	1968	1970	1972	1974	1976	1978	1980	1982	1984
Democrats	41%	41%	46%	47%	47%	44%	47%	46%	47%	51%	45%	45%	44%	40%	38%	39%	39%	41%	44%	36%
Independents	20	20	21	22	22	24	19	23	23	22	28	29	31	35	36	36	38	35	30	34
Republicans	38	38	27	27	27	29	29	27	27	24	25	24	24	23	22	23	21	22	24	28
Nothing; don't know	1	1	7	4	4	3	5	4	3	2	2	2	1	2	4	2	3	2	2	2
Total	100%	100%	101%	100%	100%	100%	100%	100%	100%	99%	100%	100%	100%	100%	100%	100%	101%	100%	100%	100%
n =	?	?	1287	1614	1139	1772	1269	3021	1317	1571	1291	1558	1507	2705	2523	2872	2283	1614	1418	1989
		(Gallup)	(NORC)				(Survey Research Center)						(Center for Political Studies)							

Sources: National Opinion Research Center; Survey Research Center, Center for Political Studies; George Gallup, *The Political Almanac, 1952* (New York: Forbes, 1952), p. 37.

TABLE 2-2 Party Identification of the Electorate for the Nation, the Non-South, and the South, 1952–1984

| | | | | | | The Nation | | | | |
	1952	1956	1960	1964	1968	1972	1976	1980	1984
Strong Democrats	22%	21%	20%	27%	20%	15%	15%	18%	17%
Weak Democrats	25	23	24	25	25	26	25	23	20
Independents	22	23	22	22	29	35	36	34	34
Weak Republicans	14	14	14	13	14	13	14	14	15
Strong Republicans	13	15	15	11	10	10	9	8	13
Apolitical, other	4	4	5	2	2	2	2	2	2
Total	100%	100%	100%	100%	100%	100%	101%	99%	101%
n =	1799	1762	1954	1571	1557	2705	2872	1614	1989

(continued)

TABLE 2-2 Continued

The Non-South

	1952	1956	1960	1964	1968	1972	1976	1980	1984
Strong Democrats	18%	17%	18%	23%	17%	13%	12%	15%	15%
Weak Democrats	22	19	20	23	24	22	22	22	18
Independents	26	26	25	25	28	37	38	37	33
Weak Republicans	16	16	16	16	17	16	17	14	17
Strong Republicans	17	18	17	12	12	12	10	9	14
Apolitical, other	2	2	4	1	1	1	2	2	2
Total	101%	98%	100%	100%	99%	101%	101%	99%	99%
n =	1290	1249	1293	1087	1076	1799	1623	1050	1352

The South

	1952	1956	1960	1964	1968	1972	1976	1980	1984
Strong Democrats	31%	29%	23%	36%	26%	17%	19%	23%	19%
Weak Democrats	32	32	33	30	28	32	30	25	23
Independents	14	15	17	15	30	29	32	29	35
Weak Republicans	8	9	8	8	8	10	11	13	11
Strong Republicans	6	8	12	8	4	9	7	7	9
Apolitical, other	9	9	6	3	2	2	2	3	3
Total	100%	102%	99%	100%	98%	99%	101%	100%	100%
n =	509	513	661	484	481	906	780	564	596

Source: Survey Research Center/Center for Political Studies National Election Studies.

North. In both the South and the North, independents hold the balance of power between Democrats and Republicans. Furthermore, the increasing tendency of southern Democrats to desert their party in presidential races means that those elections are far more competitive nationwide than the distribution of partisans would suggest.

The increase in the proportion of independents beginning in 1966 is the most interesting change reflected in these data. Wallace supporters in the South represent part of this increase, but an even larger portion are young voters who are not choosing up sides in politics as quickly as their elders did. This increase appears to have leveled off in the 1970s, but the number of independents remains at the highest point since the era of survey research began. This general loosening up of party loyalties will be further discussed later on, for it is widely suggested that it may be the forerunner of a major realignment in partisanship.

As would be expected, the likelihood of voting loyally for one party in all elections varies with the strength of partisanship of individuals. Table 2–3 shows the degree of party loyalty in presidential elections reported by the various categories of partisans. As would be expected, the independents seldom vote consistently for one party, 79 percent reporting that they have voted for presidential candidates from both parties. Strong Democratic and Republican partisans report a high degree of loyalty to their party's candidates over the years; naturally, almost no partisans have consistently voted for the other party, and only a minority have ever switched. The proportion of

TABLE 2–3 Party Regularity of Partisans and Independents in Presidential Elections, 1980

	Strong Demo- crats	Weak Demo- crats	Inde- pendents	Weak Repub- licans	Strong Repub- licans
Always voted Democratic	74%	47%	10%	1%	2%
Voted for different parties	26	53	79	71	40
Always voted Republican	0	0	10	27	58
Total	100%	100%	99%	99%	100%
n =	249	288	401	187	124

Source: Center for Political Studies 1980 National Election Study.

strong partisans who report having voted for different parties has increased substantially since 1952, when less than 10 percent of the strong Democrats and around 15 percent of the strong Republicans reported having voted for another party in past presidential elections. The defection of southern Democrats in recent presidential elections, the nomination by the Republicans in 1964 and the Democrats in 1972 of a candidate unacceptable to a large segment of his own party, and a greater general propensity to split one's ticket all have contributed to this increase.

Figure 2–2 illustrates the defections of strong and weak partisans in each presidential election since 1952. Again, declining party loyalty is apparent with a decrease in the intensity of partisanship. In most elections, strong partisans support the candidate of their party, although there are obviously differences in the appeal of candidates. Eisenhower received exceptionally large proportions of the vote from most Republicans; Goldwater received exceptionally low proportions of their vote in 1964. Among Democrats there were many defections in both 1968 and 1972. On the other hand, 1976 was a year marking a return to party loyalties with less than 10 percent of the strong partisans in both parties defecting and about 25 percent of the weak partisans supporting the candidate of the other party.

Although in 1980, and again in 1984, strong Republicans showed slightly greater party loyalty than did strong Democrats, the big difference was among weak partisans. Weak Republicans remained loyal, while one-third of the weak Democrats voted for Reagan. In 1980, an additional 7 percent of the weak Democrats voted for Anderson. Clearly, marked departures from the expected vote of a party are accomplished by wooing away the weaker partisans of the opposite party.

The tendency of both strong and weak partisans to vote according to their party identification becomes even more pronounced as one moves down the ticket to less visible and less publicized offices. Figure 2–3 shows that the voting behavior of partisans and independents in congressional races since 1952 differs from the presidential data in two significant ways. First, differences between the party loyalty of strong and weak partisans are usually smaller. Second, the defection rate does not fluctuate from year to year nearly as much as in the presidential elections, particularly among weak partisans. Both these differences are attributable to the lower visibility of congressional races. In a presidential election, the flood of available information means that a particularly attractive candidate or a stirring issue may touch the consciousness of the weak partisans, causing them to defect from

FIGURE 2-2 Defection Rates by Party Identifiers in Presidential Elections, 1952-1984

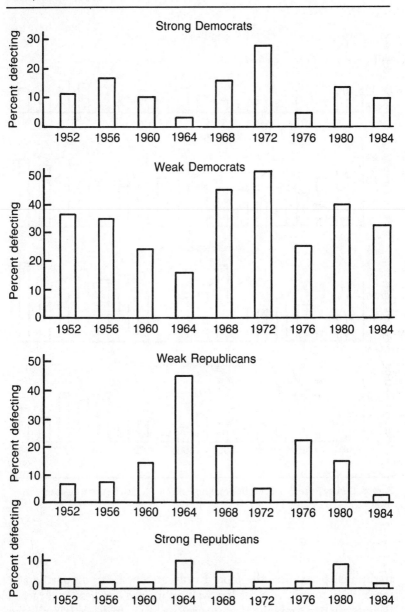

Source: Survey Research Center/Center for Political Studies National Election Studies.

FIGURE 2-3 Defection Rates by Party Identifiers in Congressional Elections, 1952–1984

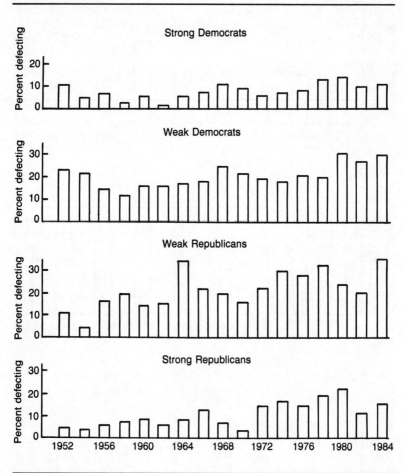

Source: Survey Research Center/Center for Political Studies National Election Studies.

traditional party ties; the more firmly attached, strong partisan is more likely to resist. In the less well-publicized congressional races, the information that might cause weak partisans to defect is less likely ever to reach them; in the absence of information about the candidates and issues, weak partisans vote their party identification.

This greater partisan stability in congressional voting can also be seen by looking at the aggregate vote for Congress. The partisan division in the vote for Congress since 1868 is shown in Figure 2–4. If one compares the congressional voting patterns in Figure 2–4 with the presidential vote in Figure 2–1, it is immediately clear that the congressional vote is considerably more stable in its partisan division than the vote for president. In addition, presidential elections show an increasing amount of variability since the end of the nineteenth century, whereas the congressional vote evidences, if anything, somewhat greater stability in the twentieth century. The higher visibility of presidential candidates and the greater availability of information about them through mass communications have led to a higher rate of defection from party lines in presidential voting. However, the increased importance of presidential races has had a different effect on candidates down the ticket: the heavy emphasis upon the presidency in the recent era has probably resulted in lower salience for congressional candidates and greater importance for partisanship and incumbency in voting decisions in congressional races.

Comparison of Figures 2–1 and 2–4 also illustrates the tendency of a victorious party in a presidential election to do less well in the next congressional election. Following the Republican presidential victories of 1952, 1956, 1972, and 1980, the Democrats increased their vote in congressional races in 1954, 1958, 1974, and 1982. In 1968, the narrow Republican presidential victory was not accompanied by a strong Republican showing in congressional races, and in 1970, the Republicans did even less well. All the other presidential elections since 1936 were Democratic victories, and in each succeeding congressional election the Republicans gained votes. The greater stability of congressional voting and the apparent return to "normal" after a presidential victory have led analysts to regard the congressional vote as more reflective of the underlying strength of the parties. Certainly it is well established that party-line voting becomes stronger for less visible offices, since issues and the personal attributes of the candidates are less likely to have an impact on the voter in less publicized races.

Actually a very significant factor in congressional elections—one often ignored by analysts—is incumbency. Studies have shown that voters are about twice as likely to be able to identify the incumbent as the challenger in congressional races and almost all the defections from partisanship are in favor of the more familiar incumbent.[4] Both

---

[4]Donald E. Stokes and Warren E. Miller, "Party Government and the Saliency of Congress," *Public Opinion Quarterly* 26 (Winter 1962).

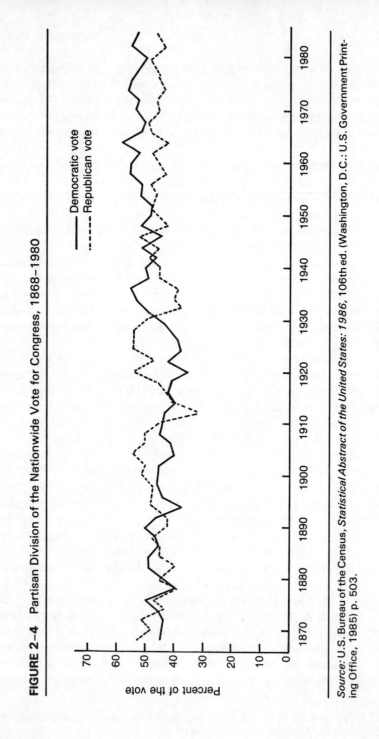

FIGURE 2–4 Partisan Division of the Nationwide Vote for Congress, 1868–1980

Democratic vote
----- Republican vote

Percent of the vote

1870 1880 1890 1900 1910 1920 1930 1940 1950 1960 1970 1980

70 60 50 40 30 20 10 0

Source: U.S. Bureau of the Census, *Statistical Abstract of the United States: 1986,* 106th ed. (Washington, D.C.: U.S. Government Printing Office, 1985) p. 503.

Republicans and Democrats seem strongly susceptible to voting for incumbents, with over one-third typically abandoning their usual party for an incumbent congressman of the other party. Strong partisans of both parties frequently defect to incumbents of the other party but on balance support the challengers from their own party more often than not. Both Democratic and Republican weak partisans, on the other hand, are more likely to defect for incumbents than to vote for challengers from their own party.

In recent decades more than 90 percent of the members of the House of Representatives have sought reelection, and all but 1 or 2 percent have survived the occasional challenges for nomination or endorsement.[5] A few incumbents are invariably defeated in the general election, but this figure rarely goes as high as 10 percent of those seeking reelection. Even in a year of stunning upsets of incumbents like 1980, only 7 percent of the incumbent members of the House of Representatives were defeated. In summary, this means that around 80 percent of the winners in congressional elections are incumbents, and the victory of incumbents, of course, means that great stability in membership exists from one Congress to the next.

This does not mean that congressional districts are invariably safe for one party, though many are. Rather, it suggests that even in those districts where the outcome is virtually a toss-up when two nonincumbents face each other, the representatives who manage to survive their first few terms soon find reelection almost assured. This tendency becomes accentuated as the opposition party finds it increasingly difficult to field an attractive candidate to challenge a secure incumbent. Thus, many incumbent representatives are elected again and again by safe margins from districts that may easily fall to the other party once the incumbent no longer seeks reelection. Put another way, the existence of a safe incumbent in a district may say little about the underlying partisan division in that district. It may simply reflect short-term forces that were at work in the last election in which two nonincumbents faced each other. Of course, the stronger the short-term forces in an election, the greater the number of congressional seats that will change hands. Basically, though, the bias in favor of incumbents means that changes in public sentiments are unlikely to be reflected quickly in changes in the composition of the House of Representatives.

---

[5]Recomputed from Barbara Hinckley, *Stability and Change in Congress* (New York: Harper & Row, 1971), p. 26.

U.S. Senators are in a somewhat different position. In the past, incumbency has been as potent an advantage for senators as for congressmen, with about 85 percent of the incumbents being returned to the Senate in an average year.[6] The election of 1976, in which 30 percent of the senators running for reelection were defeated, seems to have been indicative of a change. In 1980, the trend continued with the defeat of 39 percent of the incumbent senators seeking reelection. A Senate election has relatively high visibility and, unlike a congressional race, is amenable to a mass media campaign utilizing television. As more information about the election gets through to the voters, the less they rely upon either partisanship or the familiarity of the incumbent's name. Indeed, the very saliency of the race makes an incumbent senator vulnerable to a well-financed campaign by an attractive opponent; incumbency may, in fact, become a disadvantage in such circumstances since the incumbent has a voting record to defend.

The intensity of partisanship affects political behavior beyond its influence on the likelihood of voting for or defecting from a party's candidates. Strong partisans are also more likely to vote in all kinds of elections than either weak partisans or independents. Recall that in Chapter 1 we found that one of the most important explanations offered for the decline in turnout in recent years is the declining partisanship of the American public. Figure 2–5 shows the turnout of the various categories of partisans for three types of elections—presidential, off-year congressional, and primary elections. Presidential primaries, for all their accompanying publicity and frenetic campaigning, still had an average turnout in 1980 lower than an off-year congressional election. Turnout declines in all categories as the presumed importance of the race decreases, but the rate is much steeper among the less partisan. (Part, but by no means all, of the drop in turnout for independents in primaries is attributable to their ineligibility to vote in party primaries in some states.) As a result, the less salient the election, the more the electorate will be dominated by intense partisans, partisans who are also less likely to defect from party ties in casting their ballots.

These ideas led Angus Campbell to suggest an intriguing theory of electoral change to explain the oft-observed phenomenon in American

---

[6]Barbara Hinckley, "Incumbency and the Presidential Vote in Senate Elections: Defining Parameters of Subpresidential Voting," *American Political Science Review* 64 (September 1970): 837.

FIGURE 2-5 Turnout by Partisans and Independents in Presidential, Congressional, and Primary Elections

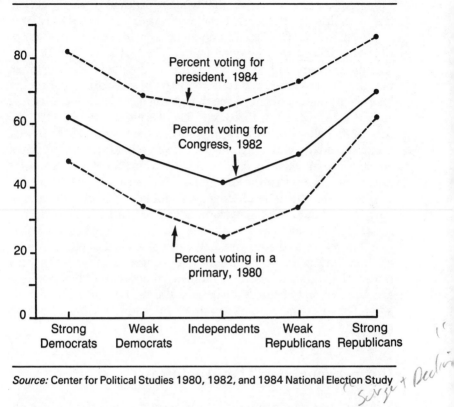

Source: Center for Political Studies 1980, 1982, and 1984 National Election Study

politics that the party winning the presidency is very likely to lose seats in the legislature in the next congressional election.[7] Because, the argument goes, presidential elections are usually accompanied by a high level of interest, large numbers of weak partisans and independents are drawn to the polls. Since these weak partisans and independents are more easily shifted from one party to another, they add disproportionately to the vote for one presidential candidate, usually the winner. In congressional elections these less committed voters do not turn out, while relatively large numbers of intense partisans do.

[7]Angus Campbell, "Surge and Decline: A Study of Electoral Change," in Campbell et al., *Elections and the Political Order* (New York: John Wiley & Sons, 1966), pp. 40–62.

These strong party identifiers are not so likely to shift their vote away from their party. Consequently, in off-year congressional elections, support declines for the party that won the previous presidential election with disproportionately large numbers of less interested voters.

Persuasive as Campbell's argument is, it rests on some assumptions that indeed may be questionable. First, it assumes that high-stimulus elections will be landslides, that is, that the short-term forces bringing the less interested voter to the polls will work to the advantage of only one candidate. Even though this often has been the case in 1952, 1956, 1964, 1972, 1980, and 1984, it is not invariable. The 1960 presidential election, with its emphasis on the religion of the Democratic candidate, was a high turnout election but different groups of voters were affected in quite different ways. Second, Campbell's argument suggests that the less interested voters who come to the polls to vote for the attractive presidential candidate will also vote for that party's candidate in congressional elections. In fact, the evidence shows that in many cases weak partisans who defect in presidential elections return to their own party in congressional elections and, in addition, independents often split their congressional vote. To some extent, the argument also rests on the assumption that independents are, in addition to being less partisan, also less informed, concerned, and interested in politics, a view that is increasingly being called into question.

Independents: Are They Apolitical?

Independents, who now account for more than one-third of the national electorate, are the most obvious source of additional votes for either party. While loyal supporters of a party sometimes abandon it—as when Democrats voted for Eisenhower in large numbers or when Republicans voted for Johnson in preference to Goldwater—year after year independents are the largest bloc of uncommitted voters available to both parties. Table 2–4 indicates the independent's capacity for shifting back and forth between the major parties. In recent years each party has, on occasion, successfully appealed to the independents, winning over a large majority to its side. In 1984, the independents voted almost two to one for Reagan over Mondale, while the Democrats held a similar advantage in 1964. The elections of 1976 and 1960 demonstrate an unpalatable fact of life for Republican presidential candidates: they must win a healthy majority of the independent vote even to stay in close contention.

TABLE 2–4 The Distribution of Votes for President by Independents, 1940–1984

	1940	1944	1948	1952	1956	1960	1964	1968	1972	1976	1980	1984
Democratic	61%	62%	57%	33%	27%	46%	66%	32%	33%	45%	26%	34%
Republican	39	38	43	67	73	54	34	47	65	55	56	66
Wallace (1968)								21				
Schmitz (1972)									2			
Anderson (1980)											14	
Other (1980)											4	
Total	100%	100%	100%	100%	100%	100%	100%	100%	100%	100%	100%	100%
n =	?	?	?	263	309	298	219	228	908	532	306	334

Source: George Gallup, *The Political Almanac,* 1952, p. 38, for data from 1940–1948, and Survey Research Center/Center for Political Studies National Election Studies for data from 1952–1984.

Third-party or independent candidates find these unaffiliated voters a major source of votes. In 1968, more than 20 percent of the independents gave their votes to Wallace; in 1980, 14 percent voted for Anderson. Put another way, more than half of Anderson's vote came from independents. Furthermore, as Figure 2–6 shows, independents may shift dramatically in voting for president and remain quite stable in voting for congressmen. Only in the post-Watergate congressional elections of 1974 was there a very one-sided pattern of independent voting.

On what basis do independents switch their party preferences? Major voting studies contend that the popular image of political independents as intelligent, informed, dispassionate evaluators of candidates, parties, and issues is mistaken. Studies from the Bureau of Applied Social Research and the Survey Research Center have supported the view that partisans of both parties are better informed and more concerned with politics than are the independents. This analysis has been reflected recently in the campaign strategies of both Democratic and Republican organizations. Increasingly, the view has become

FIGURE 2–6 Net Advantage[a] for Republicans or Democrats in Presidential and Congressional Voting among Independents, 1952–1984

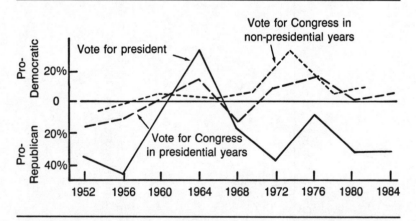

[a]The points in this figure represent the percentage of the vote given by independents to the Democrats minus the percentage they gave to the Republicans, i.e., the margin of difference between the two parties. For example, in 1978 the independent vote was 52 percent Democratic and 48 percent Republican. This appears as a 4 percent pro-Democratic percentage above the line.

Source: Survey Research Center/Center for Political Studies National Election Studies.

TABLE 2–5 Party Identifiers, Self-identified Independents, and People with No Preference, 1968–1984

In response to party identification question:	1968	1972	1976	1980	1984
Identify with a party	69%	64%	64%	64%	64%
Identify as Independents	27	28	30	24	25
Have no preference	3	8	5	12	10
Don't know	•		•		
Not ascertained	•	•	1	•	1
Total	99%	100%	100%	100%	100%
n =	1557	2702	1320	1614	1989

*Signifies less than 0.5 percent.

Source: Survey Research Center/Center for Political Studies National Election Studies.

dominant that the available voters, the voters that can be won over to either party, are an uninformed, apathetic group on whom intelligent, issue-oriented appeals and reasoned debate would be lost.

In order to pursue the analysis of independents, we need to make two distinctions that have not intruded on the discussion to this point. We will note these distinctions and then drop them because they complicate the analysis and are usually ignored.

First, there are important differences between nonpartisans who identify themselves as independents and those who lack any political identification. A sizable segment of the electorate answers the party identification question by saying they aren't anything or they don't know what they are. According to the coding conventions used by the Center for Political Studies, most of these non-identifiers are included with the independents,[8] but there may be important conceptual distinctions between them and self-identified independents. As can be seen in Table 2–5, by 1980 over one-fourth of the nonpartisans failed to identify themselves as independents. This means that by the time of the 1980 election there was a decline in the percentage of self-identified independents in the total electorate, although the overall percentage of nonpartisans remained constant. It is significant that the electorate is becoming more nonpartisan overall but less independent

---

[8]Arthur H. Miller and Martin P. Wattenberg, "Measuring Party Identification: Independent or No Partisan Preference?" *American Journal of Political Science* 27 (February 1983): 106–121.

because these situations present different implications for the political parties. Self-identified independents think of themselves as having a political identity and are somewhat anti-party in orientation. The non-identifying nonpartisans have a less clear self-image of themselves as political actors, but they are not particularly hostile to the political parties. They are less self-consciously political in many ways.

Second, within the large group of people who do not identify with a political party there are many people who say they "lean" toward either the Democratic or Republican party. These "leaners" comprise more than half of all nonpartisans and they complicate analysis in a significant way. On crucial attitudes and in important forms of political behavior, the "leaning" independents appear quite partisan. Independents who lean toward the Democratic party behave rather like weak Democratic partisans, and the same is true on the Republican side.[9] Figure 2–7 indicates that independent "leaners" are more interested in campaigns than are weak partisans, and they are as likely to vote and almost as likely to be loyal to "their party" as are weak partisans.

How appropriate, then, is it to include these individuals in one category? On some characteristics like ideological self-identification and interest in public affairs there is much more variation within the three independent categories than between the several partisan categories. The differences between "leaners" and "pure" independents are often greater than the differences between Republican and Democratic partisans. Since the concept of "independent" embraces these three dissimilar groups, there is little wonder that some disagreement exists over what the true independent is like.

As a consequence of the inclusion of these various types of people under the label "independent," it is not surprising that it is difficult to make generalizations about the degree of political interest and information independents possess. Some independents have considerable interest in politics and others are quite apathetic. There are more informed, concerned voters among the "leaning" independents than among other nonpartisans, and the "leaning" independents are more likely to register and vote. In response to our initial question, are independents attentive or apathetic toward politics? we must answer, they are some of both.

To the student of contemporary American politics, these characteristics of the independent remain important because they determine

---

[9]John Petrocik, "An Analysis of Intransitivities in the Index of Party Identification," *Political Methodology* 1 (Summer 1974): 31–47.

FIGURE 2-7 Turnout, High Interest, and Democratic Vote According to Partisanship, 1984

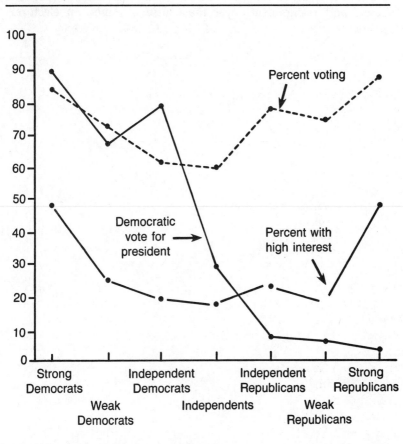

Source: Center for Political Studies 1984 National Election Study.

their susceptibility to political appeals. Many analysts have argued that the American electoral system is presently in a period of increased loosening of political ties, perhaps antecedent to a partisan realignment. The argument is that as larger and larger portions of the electorate either become independent or exhibit more independent behavior, these people form a pool of potential recruits for one of the parties, or a new party. Should one of the parties be able to capture the imagination of this pool of available recruits, it could lead to a significant change in the partisan division in the electorate. We will return to this theme in Chapter 4 as we consider the issues of partisan change and realignments over the course of American electoral history.

3

Social Characteristics of Partisans and Independents

☆ ☆ ☆

To this point the voting behavior and political partisanship of Americans have been discussed without examination of the forces behind these patterns. The major attempts to explain American voting behavior have relied on social and economic factors to account for both stability and change in American politics. The major studies of the Survey Research Center and the Center for Political Studies have documented a wide range of relationships in the American electorate between social and economic characteristics and political behavior. Furthermore, social and economic factors form the basis of many descriptions of voting patterns by American journalists and party strategists. Analysis regularly attributes political trends to a "farm revolt" or "fixed-income groups"; frequently these explanations rely on so-called bloc voting, like "the black vote," "the Catholic vote," "the union vote," implying that some social factor causes large numbers of people to vote the same way.

Most commonly, these explanations focus on the association between social status and partisan choice. Typically, it is said that working-class people, blue-collar workers, those with low educational levels, those with low incomes, ethnic groups of more recent immigration, racial minorities, and Catholics are more likely to vote Democratic than are higher status people—middle-class individuals, those

49

with white-collar occupations, the college educated, those with high incomes, whites, Protestants, and those of northern European stock.

Although all these relationships exist and are important for understanding and interpreting American political behavior, one must be careful not to overstate the case, for any *single* social or economic characteristic is not likely to be a very good predictor of how an individual will behave politically. For example, even though those in white-collar occupations are more likely to be Republicans than are blue-collar workers, there are equal numbers of white-collar Democrats and white-collar Republicans. The differences are similarly unimpressive for most other socioeconomic variables taken alone mainly because the groups defined by each of these variables are, in the United States, quite heterogeneous with respect to other variables. For example, even though white-collar workers on the average are better off than blue-collar workers, white-collar workers range from wealthy physicians to starving artists, and blue-collar workers include such diverse types as highly skilled and well-paid artisans and part-time cleaning crews; and both contain individuals of widely varying educational levels, religious- and ethnic-group membership, and so on. The same can be said about other social and economic variables. The one exception to this is race. Because of the systematic discrimination against blacks in American culture, blacks form a much more homogeneous group socioeconomically, as well as a more politically self-conscious one, than most other groups in American society. It is not surprising, then, that their political behavior is also more homogeneous.

The ability to predict the political behavior of whites from their social and economic characteristics is increased if several variables are combined. In effect, more and more homogeneous groups are being created for analysis in this manner, and such groups are increasingly likely to behave in similar ways. Figure 3–1 displays the partisanship of selected socioeconomic groups in 1952 and 1984, revealing a tendency for Democratic identification to decline with increasing education. Among white Protestants and Catholics of all educational levels in the North, the comparison of 1984 with 1952 shows a gain in the proportions of independents at the expense of both parties but otherwise a relatively stable pattern of party identification. These categories, of course, include the bulk of the population. Southern whites have become dramatically less Democratic over these thirty-two years. Blacks in both regions have become slightly more Democratic and since 1964 have been the most consistently loyal Democratic group. Although Jews shifted away from their extremely one-sided

FIGURE 3-1 Party Identification According to Region, Race, Religion, and Education, 1952 and 1984

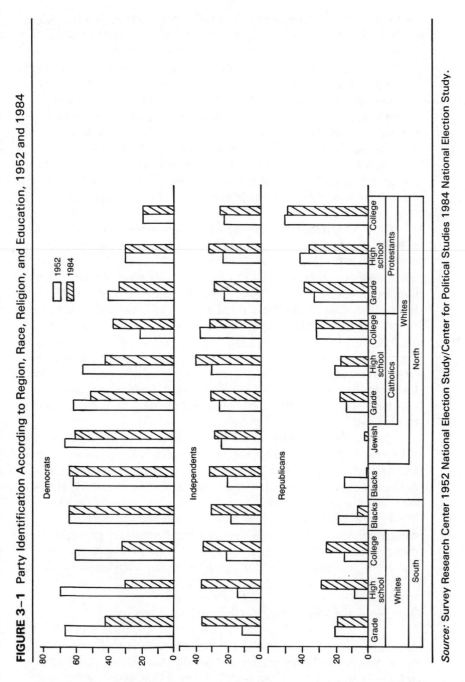

Source: Survey Research Center 1952 National Election Study/Center for Political Studies 1984 National Election Study.

Democratic identification in the 1970s, by the 1980s they were once again as heavily Democratic and as seldom Republican as they had been in the early 1950s.

One factor that is often important in explaining political behavior and yet complicates simple social and economic interpretations is the nature of the community or the region in which the individual lives. Sometimes the culture and traditions of an area will reverse or reinforce the political tendencies of other social groupings to which the individual belongs; this may result in a pattern of behavior different from that of people with similar characteristics in other parts of the country. Unless the analyst controls for such "contextual" factors, finding any common patterns in the group's behavior may be difficult.

The most obvious example of such a regional effect is the division between the South and the rest of the nation. The South has been overwhelmingly Democratic since the Civil War, and for years this traditional attachment to the Democratic party virtually wiped out the impact of any other social or economic factor on political behavior. In the 1950s, the southern middle class was about as Democratic as the southern working class, the highly educated about as Democratic as the less well educated, southern Protestants as Democratic as the relatively few Catholics in that region, and so on. If the analyst failed to separate Southerners from the rest of the population in investigating political behavior, the substantial relationship found between religion, education, and class in other parts of the nation would be obscured.

Controlling for region, as in Figure 3–1, is relatively simple. It is not such an easy matter to take community effects into account, since national surveys may contain very little information about community characteristics and very few cases from any one community. However, community traditions may have substantial impact. For example, Italian-Americans in some New England and upstate New York cities traditionally have been Republicans; their social group influence is strong, and yet it moves group members in the opposite direction from that taken by similar group influences elsewhere.

The Social Composition of Partisan Groups

Another way of looking at the relationship between socioeconomic characteristics and partisanship is to describe the Democratic and Republican parties and independents in terms of proportions of different kinds of individuals who make up their ranks. Figure 3–2 illustrates the composition of Democratic, Republican, and independent identifiers using the same social categories as were introduced in Figure 3–1, that is, region, race, religion, and education. Note, however, that this way of looking at the data gives different results and answers a different set of questions. For example, when one looked at the partisanship of various social groups in Figure 3–1, Jews were found to be heavily Democratic; in 1984, 62 percent of the Jewish respondents called themselves Democrats. On the other hand, if one calculates the proportion of all Democrats who are Jews, as in Figure 3–2, one finds that Jews make up less than 5 percent of the total group of Democrats. Because Jews are small in number, although quite homogeneous politically, they contribute relatively few voters to the Democratic party compared with the voter contributions of other larger, though less loyal, groups.

Studying the partisanship of various social groups has generally been regarded as the more interesting way of looking at the relationship between social characteristics and political behavior, largely because of the causal connection between partisanship and social characteristics. Thus one is far more inclined to say that region, race, religion, or education "causes" an individual to select a particular political party than to say that political affiliation "causes" any of the others. On the other hand, familiarity with the composition of the parties is useful in understanding the campaign strategies and political appeals that the parties make in order to hold their supporters in line and sway the independents or opposition supporters to their side. For example, the need of the Democrats to hold the South in the Democratic coalition, as well as the opportunity the South offers Republicans, is revealed by the fact that white Southerners contribute almost one-quarter of the total Democratic strength in the electorate. Similarly, the fact that blacks contribute 20 percent of the Democratic partisans but make up only 2 percent of the Republican identifiers is a significant factor that both parties must take into account.

As Figure 3–2 demonstrates, the composition of the partisan identifiers is distinctively different: many groups make a sizeable contribution to the Democratic following yet very few social groups constitute a significant share of the Republican. As a category, Republicans are much more homogeneous, consisting of relatively well-educated white Protestants from the South and North.

Even though the Democrats are considerably more varied in social composition than the Republicans, the main conclusion to be drawn from an analysis of the partisan groupings is their basic hetero-

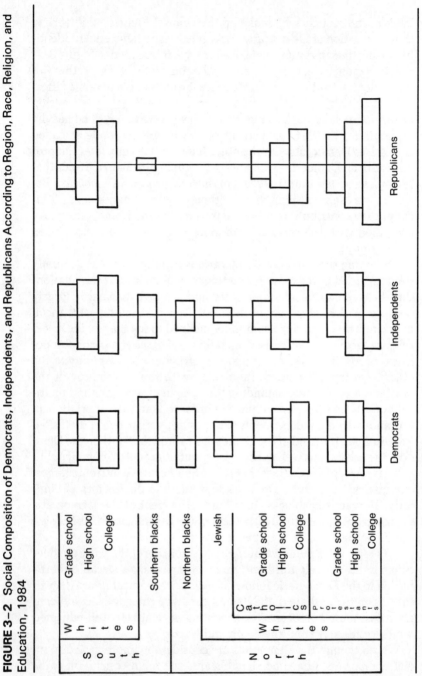

FIGURE 3–2 Social Composition of Democrats, Independents, and Republicans According to Region, Race, Religion, and Education, 1984

Source: Center for Political Studies 1984 National Election Study.

54

geneity. Both parties contain substantial proportions of differing religious groups and people with different educational levels; they both draw substantial portions of their votes from blue-collar workers and white-collar workers, from the young, the middle-aged, the old, and so on. Thus, with few exceptions, neither party can ignore any reasonably large social group. This, perhaps as much as any factor, forces the parties to take moderate and largely similar positions on most social issues.

Social Group Analysis

The impact of social groups on individual behavior is so commonly understood and accepted that it needs little elaboration, and the forms of group influence are too varied to discuss them all. Social analysis of political behavior has examined mainly three units: primary groups, secondary groups, and social classes. Briefly, these terms have the following meanings: *Primary groups* are the face-to-face groups with whom one associates, like family, friends, and fellow workers. *Secondary groups* are organizations or collections of individuals with whom one identifies or is identified but have some common interest or goal rather than personal contact as their major basis. *Social classes* are broad groupings based on position in society according to social status.

PRIMARY GROUPS

Although investigations of the political behavior of primary groups are not numerous, all available evidence indicates that families and groups of friends are very likely to be politically homogeneous. Groups of workers appear somewhat more mixed politically. Presumably, the social forces in families and friendship groups are more intense and more likely to be based on, or to result in, political unanimity, but in most work situations people are thrown together without an opportunity to form groups based on common political values or any other shared traits. Friendship groups, even casual ones, may be formed so that individuals with much in common, including political views, naturally come together.

Table 3–1 reproduces a set of findings originally presented by Campbell, Converse, Miller, and Stokes in *The American Voter* from their 1952 national survey. These data on the voter's primary groups do not reflect the indecisiveness of some voters or the extent to which

TABLE 3–1 Relation of Reported Partisan Preferences of Primary Groups to Respondent's Own Partisan Choice, 1952[a]

Respondent Voted	Spouse Voted		Family Voted[b]		Friends Voted		Work Associates Voted	
	Dem.	Rep.	Dem.	Rep.	Dem.	Rep.	Dem.	Rep.
Democratic	89%	7%	80%	8%	83%	15%	79%	24%
Republican	11	93	20	92	17	85	21	76
Total	100%	100%	100%	100%	100%	100%	100%	100%
n[c] =	337	496	75	108	355	574	271	290

Notes: [a]This tabulation is limited to persons who reported voting for a major party candidate for president and who could attribute to the primary group in question a clear partisan preference.
[b]Asked only of unmarried respondents.
[c]Includes a small number of persons who voted for a minor party candidate.

Source: Angus Campbell et al., *The American Voter* (New York: John Wiley & Sons, 1960), p. 77, Table 4.3.

primary groups have mixed or unknown voting preferences. Nevertheless, where an individual is aware of a partisan preference, that preference is extremely likely to correspond with his or her own. Although these data are now over thirty years old, the findings are so plausible that no major studies have reexamined the basic conclusion.

The word *conformity* to describe this pattern of primary-group behavior has been avoided because these group processes are more casual and more a matter of give-and-take than use of the term *conformity* would imply. Most people care very little about politics, and it plays a small part in their personal relations. In very few primary groups is politics of any consequence, so the things that happen in the group leading to political homogeneity are of low salience. One gradually creates, evaluates, and revises an image of the world under the influence of social pressures, many of these processes being face-to-face exchanges of information or reassurances that someone else shares views or considers them plausible, realistic, and acceptable. Most individuals are not "pressured" by primary groups to conform or to change politically, at least not nearly as much as they are influenced by casual, impromptu expressions of similar ideas and values. Ordinarily, primary groups do not tolerate high levels of political tension and conflict. Also, very few people are subject to the social forces of only one or two primary groups, so conformity to group pressure would mean conformity to a large number of groups.

In addition to what happens within primary groups, another factor produces political similarity: the likelihood that primary-group members share the same social background and experiences outside the group. Members of any primary group are very apt to be socially, economically, ethnically, and racially alike, and being alike in these ways means that the same general social influences are at work on them. Much happens outside the primary group to make it politically homogeneous.

SECONDARY GROUPS

Secondary groups form the level of social organization between primary groups and social classes. This covers a range of groups in society like labor unions, religious or fraternal organizations, and professional groups. Secondary groups are presumably composed of overlapping primary groups whose pressures toward political homogeneity spill over, tending to make the members of secondary groups alike. In addition, the members of secondary groups are likely to be subject to the same social forces outside the group. For example, members of a labor union are likely to be in the same income group, to live in the same type of neighborhood, and to have the same social and educational background, all of which would tend to make them alike politically.

A third factor at work is the role that a secondary group may play as a reference group. A group serves as a reference group for an individual who uses the group as a guide in forming opinions. For example, if union members, identifying with their labor union, perceive that a particular policy is good for the union, perhaps because the union leadership says that it is, and favor the policy because of this, then the union is a political reference group for those individuals. In the same way, if a union member believes that other union members support a policy and supports the policy partially for this reason, the union members serve as a reference group. Also, if a white-collar worker perceives that unions favor a policy and opposes it in part for that reason, the union serves as a negative reference group.

The most sophisticated analysis of social groups and political behavior applied to national survey data appeared some years ago in *The American Voter*.[1] By controlling many outside social influences with matched groups, the authors demonstrated the degree to which political behavior is influenced by secondary-group membership among union members, blacks, Catholics, and Jews. They were able to show that these groups, except for Catholics, were considerably more Democratic than one would expect from the group members' other social characteristics, such as urban-rural residence, region, and occupational status. Even greater influence was present if the individual identified with the group. In order to establish the importance of identification with the group and belief in the legitimacy of the group's involvement in politics, the authors of *The American Voter* analyzed the presidential votes of union members, blacks, Catholics, and Jews. The increasing impact of identification with the group and its perceived legitimacy was associated with an increasing Democratic vote. In other words, the stronger the belief in the legitimacy of the group's political involvement and the stronger the group identification, the greater the impact of group standards on vote choice.

Among groups usually studied, blacks and Jews remain to the present the most distinctive politically. Union members, in contrast, have been extremely volatile in voting for president in recent elec-

---

[1]Angus Campbell et al., *The American Voter* (New York: John Wiley & Sons, 1960), pp. 295–332.

tions. Union members abandoned their strong pro-Democratic leanings in 1968 when a majority of them failed to support Hubert Humphrey, who was certainly considered to have great appeal for labor. Another defection from Democratic loyalties comparable in magnitude occurred in 1972, when union members supported Nixon over McGovern by a 3-to-2 margin. In 1976, union members returned to the Democratic candidate with a margin approaching 2 to 1. By 1980, union members' support for Carter had eroded and a bare majority backed him for president. This pattern continued in 1984 when Mondale only narrowly outpolled Reagan in union households. The behavior of union members in 1972 and 1976 might well be examples of the importance of unions as reference groups for their members since union leadership also departed from traditional Democratic loyalties in 1972, returning to them in 1976. However, 1984 represented a major failure for union leaders as they strongly committed themselves and their unions' resources to Mondale without much influence on their rank and file.

An example of more homogeneous group behavior was revealed by the black community in 1984 in its response to the appeals of Jesse Jackson. Even though many blacks voted for Mondale in the primaries, there was a widespread response to the themes of the Jackson campaign. Furthermore, Jackson's leadership generated a certain amount of activity within black neighborhoods to register new voters and to become better organized politically.

The voting patterns of American religious groups usually are not particularly distinctive, or at least other factors are considered more important in determining vote choice. The 1960 presidential election provides a good example of how secondary groups become relevant in a particular election and temporarily have great influence on voting behavior. Kennedy's Catholicism was a major issue throughout the campaign and of great salience to both Catholics and non-Catholics.

The researchers at the University of Michigan separated Protestant Democrats according to frequency of church attendance and compared each subgroup's defection from Kennedy by calculating the normal defection of the group as a whole.[2] Figure 3–3 shows their findings. In both the South and North, Protestant Democrats who were more regular in church attendance were more likely to defect from the Democratic party. Among the nominal Protestants who never attended church, Kennedy's Catholicism had no such impact.

---

[2]Angus Campbell et al., *Elections and the Political Order* (New York: John Wiley & Sons, 1966), chap. 5.

FIGURE 3-3 Defection to Nixon among Protestant Democrats as a Function of Church Attendance[a]

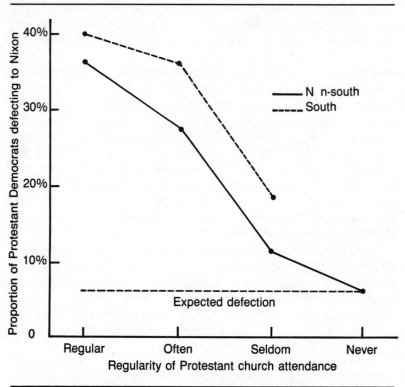

[a]The number of Protestant Democrats who "never" attend church in the South is too small for inclusion.

Source: Angus Campbell et al., *Elections and the Political Order* (New York: John Wiley & Sons, 1966), p. 89, Figure 5.1.

With a "born-again Christian" in the contest, the 1976 presidential election afforded speculation that religion might again be an important factor in the outcome. Figure 3–4 shows the departure from expected Democratic voting according to regularity of church attendance among southern fundamentalists, a group that presumably would find Carter's message most appealing. Surprisingly, the pattern is the opposite of what might be expected. The most regular church-goers among the southern fundamentalists were more likely to

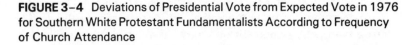

FIGURE 3–4 Deviations of Presidential Vote from Expected Vote in 1976 for Southern White Protestant Fundamentalists According to Frequency of Church Attendance

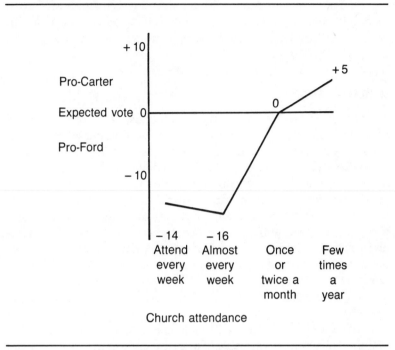

Source: Center for Political Studies/1976 National Election Study.

desert Carter for Ford than the less faithful attenders. In 1976 and again in 1980, the moderately liberal stance that Carter took on a number of social issues apparently outweighed whatever appeal a co-religionist might have held for these southern fundamentalists. This finding could be repeated for other religious groups, North and South.

Although the evidence is meager on this point, political analysts believe that the temporary salience of the religious issue as in 1960 and the sharper drawing of social lines around religious boundaries are typical of what happens to many social factors occasionally. A social factor, like religion or union membership or Italian ancestry or wheat farming, after years of dormancy may temporarily become important during a political campaign and subsequently again becomes unimportant. This irregular rising and falling of issues dramatizing social groups is a partial explanation for the political heterogeneity of American social groups. If the issues dramatizing a given social group were constantly salient, one would expect partisan realignment on the basis of membership or nonmembership in that group. But if the group is politically salient for only one campaign or so, such major realignment does not occur. Presumably, as such issues are raised there is some partisan movement; but the changing salience of groups leads to political heterogeneity rather than to pure divisions.

SOCIAL CLASSES

A third major focus of analysis is social class. Some of the leading hypotheses of social and political theory link social classes and political behavior. Generally, the expectations surrounding social class include these: (1) differences exist in the economic and social interests of social classes, and (2) these conflicting interests will be translated into political forces. The critical variable in this view appears to be the importance of social class interests. In American society the importance of social class fluctuates but never becomes extremely high. The major political and sociological theories of social class have taken for granted the supreme importance of class interests, an assumption that seems unrealistic in American society. About one-third of all American adults say that they never think of themselves as members of a social class.

Given a choice between "middle class" and "working class," a majority of Americans are able to place themselves in a general social position, even to the point of including themselves in the "upper" or "lower" level of a class. Even though individual self-ratings are not perfectly congruent with the positions that social analysts would assign those individuals on the basis of characteristics like occupation, income, and education, a general social class structure is apparent. The political significance of social class varies from election to election in much the same way as that of secondary groups. Figure 3–5 shows the relationship between self-identification as a member of the working or middle class and party identification from 1952 through 1984 in the nation as a whole and in the North and South. The values on the graph line represent the strength of the relationship between social class and party. If all working-class people identified with the Democratic party and all middle-class people were Republicans (with the independents split evenly between the two parties), the strength of the relationship would be +1.0; if the reverse were true, the relationship would be -1.0. If there were no differences in the partisan prefer-

FIGURE 3-5 The Relationship between Social Class Identification and Party Identification, 1952-1984

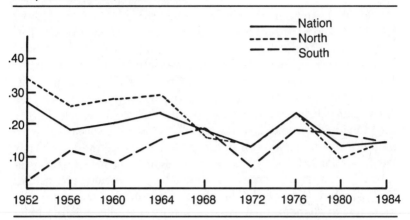

Note: The coefficients represented by points on the graph are Somer's d.

Source: Survey Research Center/Center for Political Studies National Election Studies.

ences of middle- and working-class people, the relationship would be 0.0. Because working-class people have been more likely to be Democrats than have middle-class people in each year since 1952, all the values in Figure 3-5 are positive.

A number of points can be made about the data in Figure 3-5. Although the strength of the relationship between social class and party has varied over the years, the national trend in the relationship is downward. In other words, since 1952 the differences in partisan preference between working- and middle-class people are getting smaller. In this context, 1976 stands out as a sharp, if temporary, reversal of the trend before a new low was reached in 1980. It is also clear from Figure 3-5 that the relationship between class and party has followed quite different patterns in North and South. Whereas the relationship is steadily declining in the North, it has actually increased in the South. In the early 1950s in the South, middle- and working-class people were overwhelmingly Democratic; there were virtually no differences between them. Since that time, a modest, class-based partisan alignment has emerged in the South. The middle class has become increasingly Republican, while the working class, particularly the black working class, remains quite solidly Democratic. By 1984, the class alignment in the South was virtually identical to that of the

North, although in both regions the class basis of partisanship was weak.

Another common expectation about the relationship between social class and partisanship has to do with upward and downward social mobility. To put it simply, the argument has been that upwardly mobile individuals abandon a Democratic identification and become Republicans, whereas the downwardly mobile abandon the Republican party to become Democrats. And, during the period of maximum social and political stress associated with this mobility, presumably the individual becomes an independent. It has not been easy to assess mobility at a national level in the United States, so the surprisingly weak relationship usually found may result from inadequate measurement. In broad terms, most members of society are neither upwardly nor downwardly mobile, and the socially mobile seem no more apt to abandon their parents' loyalty than the socially stable. There is, in fact, very little political difference between the upwardly and downwardly mobile, and this appears to hold for several measures of mobility.

Along with Canada, the United States is usually regarded as an extreme case among developed democracies for the insignificance of social class in political behavior; in most European democracies social class is of greater consequence.[3] Two factors may depress the apparent relationship between social class and voting behavior in the United States. Aggregating data for the entire population has been shown to hide stronger relationships in subgroups and in particular communities.[4] Probably more important is the tendency of American political leaders not to emphasize highly divisive social class lines. Social class may serve as a political guide for some citizens on certain issues, but it does not appear to be extremely important in American politics.

---

[3]There are several important works on social class and political behavior in addition to Campbell et al.'s *The American Voter*, chap. 13. Students interested in this area of analysis should see Robert Alford, *Party and Society* (Chicago: Rand McNally and Company, 1963); and Richard Rose (ed.), *Electoral Behavior* (New York: The Free Press, 1974). Perhaps the most significant work is David Butler and Donald E. Stokes, *Political Change in Britain: Forces Shaping Electoral Choice* (New York: St. Martin's Press, 1969).

[4]For example, in 1968 in Minnesota the relationship between class and party approached the level found in Western European countries. William H. Flanigan and Robert E. Crew, "Minnesota," *Explaining the Vote: Presidential Choices in the Nation and the States, 1968*, ed. David M. Kovenock, James W. Prothro, et al. (Chapel Hill, N.C.: Institute for Research in Social Science, 1974).

Social Cross-Pressures

One of the major ideas developed in the early voting studies by Lazarsfeld, Berelson, and other researchers at the Bureau of Applied Social Research of Columbia University was the "cross-pressure hypothesis."[5] The cross-pressure hypothesis is simple in outline, but it can be confusing because it takes so many different forms. The hypothesis concerns the situation in which two (or more) forces or tendencies act on the individual, one in a Republican direction and the other in a Democratic direction. Sometimes this is stated as two factors predisposing a voter in a Republican or a Democratic direction. Usually the hypothesis is presented with two social dimensions, like occupation and religion, as in the box below.

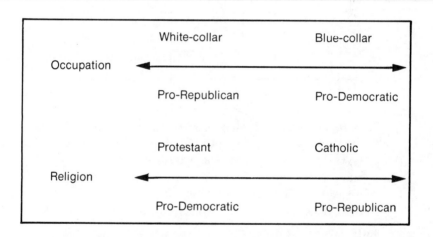

Some individuals are predisposed or pushed in a consistent way, such as white-collar Protestants, whose occupation and religion both. predispose them in a Republican direction, or blue-collar Catholics predisposed in a Democratic direction.

---

[5]Paul Lazarsfeld, Bernard Berelson, and Hazel Gaudet, *The People's Choice* (New York: Columbia University Press, 1944); Bernard Berelson, Paul Lazarsfeld, and William McPhee, *Voting* (Chicago: University of Chicago Press, 1954).

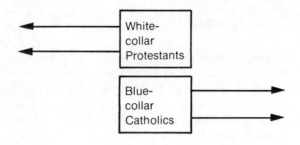

But some individuals are predisposed in both directions, or "cross-pressured."

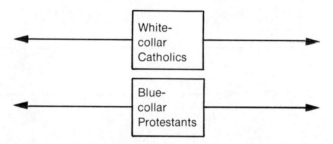

The cross-pressure hypothesis asserts that individuals under consistent pressure behave differently from individuals under cross-pressure. The predictions under the hypothesis are:

Consistent Pressure	Cross-Pressure
straight-ticket voting	split-ticket voting
early decision on vote	late decision on vote
high interest in politics	low interest in politics
high level of information	low levels of information
consistent attitudes	conflicting attitudes

These expectations about voting behavior under cross-pressure are actually specific applications of more general patterns investigated by sociologists and psychologists in a variety of ways. The responses to cross-pressure predicted by the hypothesis are avoidance reactions—efforts to avoid or to minimize the anxiety produced by conflict.

The cross-pressure hypothesis has some implications for empirical political theory also. According to the cross-pressure hypothesis many large social groups are expected to be stable politically; that is, they are consistently predisposed to be Republican or Democratic by the social forces working on them. Therefore, these social pressures lead to political stability among both Republicans and Democrats because they have politically consistent social backgrounds.

Between these politically consistent social groups there are cross-pressured groups predisposed toward both parties. According to the cross-pressure thesis, these groups are politically unstable, contributing the voters who switch from one party to another. This means that the available voters, the voters to whom the parties must appeal in order to win because they hold the balance of power in elections, are in a middle position between Democrats and Republicans.

These arguments lead to a reassuring view of the American electorate. There is widespread political stability based on a relatively stable social system. Political flexibility and sensitivity are provided by groups in between the partisans who are therefore politically moderate. As long as the stable partisan groups are roughly of the same size, stable competitive conditions are guaranteed. As long as social groups overlap somewhat, the necessary cross-pressures will exist to produce the switching political moderates. It appears to be an electoral system with no weaknesses.

Nevertheless, there are some difficulties with this picture of the electoral system. For one thing, the social cross-pressure thesis is merely a tendency and not a perfect description of the impact of social forces on political behavior. The politically stable are more heterogeneous than the above account implies, and the politically flexible are not under dramatic social cross-pressure, according to the best data available.

Discussion supporting the cross-pressure thesis is most extensive in the Elmira study, *Voting*, by Berelson, Lazarsfeld, and McPhee. They found that cross-pressures affect the time when an individual decides how to vote. There was a slight tendency for cross-pressures caused by religion and socioeconomic status to be associated with late decisions on voting. There were stronger relationships associated with conflicts in primary groups.

It is possible to conceptualize social cross-pressure as leading to cross-pressure on political attitudes that in turn leads to the predicted patterns of behavior. Actually, attitudinal cross-pressure is the only form of cross-pressure that is strongly confirmed by national survey data. When attitudes toward the candidates and parties were measured by the Survey Research Center in 1952 and 1956, conflicting attitudes—those of an individual holding pro-Democratic and pro-Republican opinions—were associated with nonvoting, indecision, and indifference toward the election. These findings linking conflicting political attitudes with patterns of behavior have not always been confirmed in subsequent election studies, depending on exactly which attitudes are examined. Nevertheless, it remains reasonable to expect conflicting political attitudes to be associated with indecisiveness in voting behavior.

The American electoral system appears to operate in a way predicted by the cross-pressure hypothesis. There is partisan stability among both Republicans and Democrats, and the shifting of political fortunes is accomplished without intensity or extreme political appeals. One should, however, be skeptical of explaining these political patterns as a result of the social forces postulated by the cross-pressure thesis. Neither short-run partisan stability nor independent flexibility appears strongly associated with social-group predispositions. Two conclusions can be drawn about social characteristics and voting behavior. On the one hand, social factors, like race, religion, and occupation, as well as primary groups, have been shown to be related to partisanship. The long-run social and political patterns in the American electorate appear related. On the other hand, the short-run impact of social groups on voting behavior appears uneven and generally insignificant. Occasionally, social forces appear important nationally, as religion did in 1960, and under certain conditions social cross-pressure may operate. However, normally social factors are not expected to show the same consistent, strong relationship with vote choice that was found in the case of partisanship.

4

Partisan Change

★★★

The concept of partisanship can be thought of as establishing a normal
or "expected" vote, an estimate about how individuals or populations
will vote, other things being equal. Such an estimate can be used as a
baseline against which short-term defections can be measured and
analyzed. For example, in the preceding two chapters, we used party
identification to analyze the defections of various categories of partisans, born-again Christians and union members, in various elections.

However, as implied in references to the contemporary period,
partisanship itself is not unchangeable. Individuals may change, not
only their vote, but their long-term party identification from one
party to another. More importantly, over extended periods of time,
the partisan composition of the electorate may be altered as new voters of one political persuasion replace older voters of another. When
the basic partisan division of the electorate changes, it is called a *partisan realignment*.

In this chapter, we will examine the partisan division of the electorate historically, the major realignments that have occurred, and
the processes that have brought about these patterns. Then we will
look at the evidence of changes in partisanship in the contemporary
period and assess the likelihood that a partisan realignment is currently underway.

Expected Voting Patterns

In order to assess the partisanship of the American electorate historically, we base our estimates on the only available data—election returns for aggregate units.[1] These data cannot, of course, reveal the voting patterns of individuals; they do, however, allow one to make assessments of the party loyalty and temporary deviations from party by collections of voters. Even though not exactly the same set of individuals turns out to vote in each election, we use the election returns over the years to indicate the collective partisanship of the electorate. From these data, an estimate is made of the normal or "expected" vote for the Democratic and the Republican parties. It is then possible to say, for example, that the electorate deviated from its normal voting pattern in favor of the Republican party in 1904 or that the voters departed somewhat from their normal Democratic loyalty in 1952.

Figure 4-1 presents our estimates of the expected vote nationwide in presidential voting for the Democratic party from 1840 to the present and for the Republican party from 1872 to the present. The actual vote in these elections is also shown to indicate the amount of departure from underlying partisan patterns that occurred in each election.

Types of Electoral Change

As we have said, the utility of the concept of the expected vote lies, in part, in providing a base against which to measure and analyze departures from the expected pattern. One type of departure is usually referred to as *deviating change:* the temporary deviations from normal party loyalty occasioned by the short-term forces of candidate images or issues.[2] The amount of deviating change in an election tells how well a candidate or party did relative to the party's normal performance. In these terms, the Eisenhower victories or the Nixon landslide appear even more dramatic because they represent big Republican margins during a time when the Democratic party held an

---

[1]This discussion and data presentation are based on our earlier work in William H. Flanigan and Nancy H. Zingale, "The Measurement of Electoral Change," *Political Methodology* 1 (Summer 1974).

[2]This and most discussions of the classification of elections are based on the work of V. O. Key and Angus Campbell. V. O. Key, "A Theory of Critical Elections," *Journal of Politics* 17 (1955), pp. 3–18; and Angus Campbell, "A Classification of Presidential Elections," in Campbell et al., *Elections and the Political Order* (New York: John Wiley & Sons, 1966), pp. 63–77.

advantage in party loyalists. These "deviating elections" involved substantial departures from the underlying strength of the two parties in the electorate.

These temporary deviating changes may be dramatic and reflect important electoral forces, but another type of change is of even greater interest. On rare occasions in American national politics a permanent or *realigning change* in voting patterns occurs. In such an instance, the electorate departs from its existing expected voting pattern but does not thereafter return to the old pattern. On occasion these changes are large enough to alter the competitive balance among the parties with significant consequences for the policy directions of government. Such a period of change is usually referred to as a *partisan realignment*.[3]

Electoral analysts usually discuss three major realignments in American history: one accompanied the Civil War and the emergence of the Republican party, another followed the depression of 1893 and benefited the Republicans, and the most recent followed the depression of 1929 and led to Democratic party dominance. These abrupt changes in the expected votes of the parties can be seen in Figures 4–1 *a* and *b*. Each realignment of partisan loyalties coincided with a major national crisis, leading to the supposition that a social or economic crisis is necessary to shake loose customary loyalties. But major crises and national traumas have not always led to disruptions of partisanship, suggesting that other political conditions must also be present in order for a crisis to produce a realignment. The nature of the realignment crisis has political significance, however, for it generally determines the lines along which the rearrangement in partisan loyalties will take place, as different segments of the electorate respond differently to the crisis and to attempts to solve it.

In general, realignments appear to happen in the following way. At a time of national crisis, the electorate rejects the party in power, giving a decisive victory to the other party, a victory that includes not only the presidency but large majorities in both houses of Congress. Armed with this political mandate, the new party in office acts to meet the crisis, often with innovative policies that are sharp departures from the past. *If* the administration's policy initiatives are successful in solving the nation's problems (or at least are widely perceived as successful), then significant numbers of voters will become

---

[3]This and the following discussion draws heavily on Jerome M. Clubb, William H. Flanigan, and Nancy H. Zingale, *Partisan Realignment: Voters, Parties and Government in American History* (Beverly Hills, Calif.: Sage Publications, 1980).

FIGURE 4–1a Democratic Expected Vote in Presidential Elections, 1840–1984

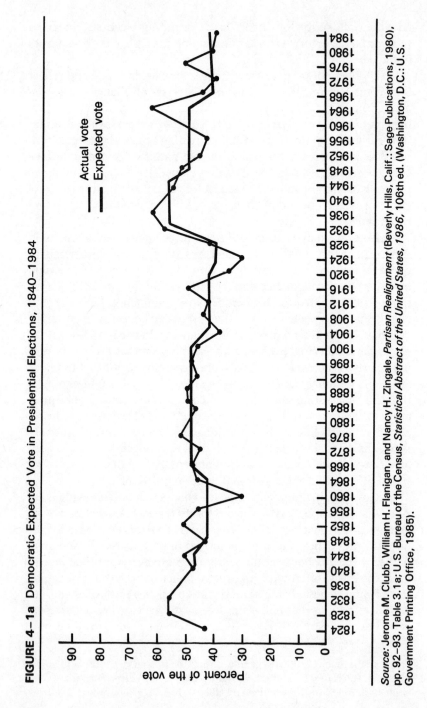

Source: Jerome M. Clubb, William H. Flanigan, and Nancy H. Zingale, *Partisan Realignment* (Beverly Hills, Calif.: Sage Publications, 1980), pp. 92–93, Table 3.1a; U.S. Bureau of the Census, *Statistical Abstract of the United States, 1986,* 106th ed. (Washington, D.C.: U.S. Government Printing Office, 1985).

72

FIGURE 4–1b Republican Expected Vote in Presidential Elections, 1872–1984

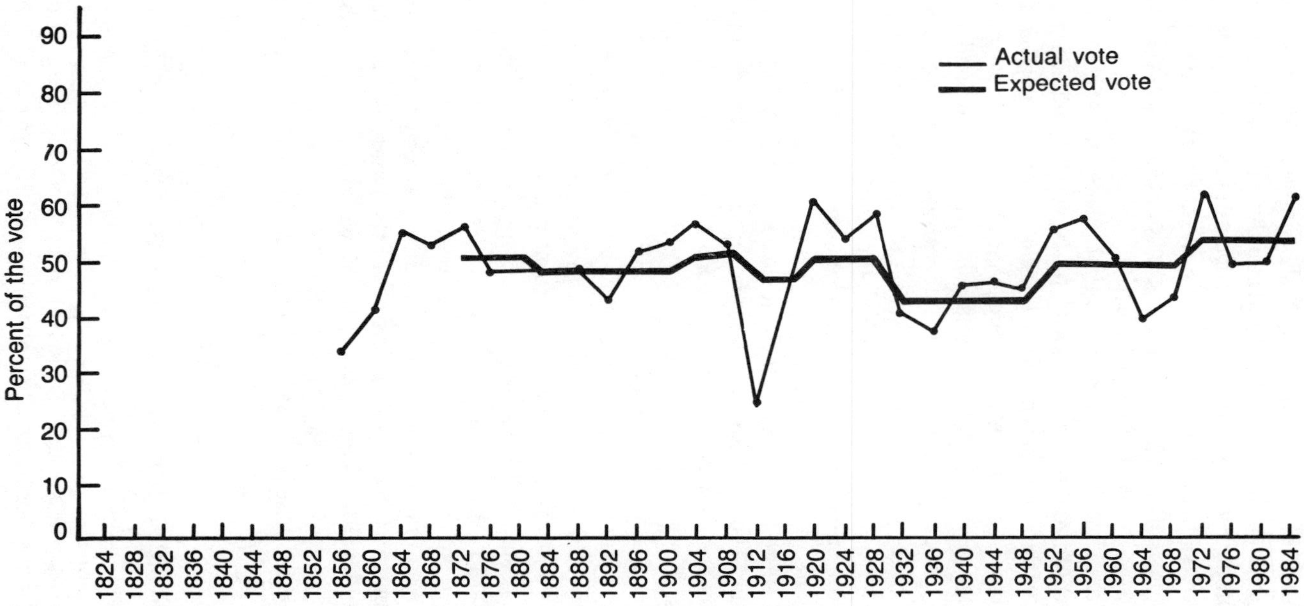

Source: Jerome M. Clubb, William H. Flanigan, and Nancy H. Zingale, *Partisan Realignment* (Beverly Hills, Calif.: Sage Publications, 1980), pp. 92–93, Table 3.1a; U.S. Bureau of the Census, *Statistical Abstract of the United States, 1986,* 106th ed. (Washington, D.C.: U.S. Government Printing Office, 1985).

73

partisans of the new administration's party and continue voting for it in subsequent elections, thus causing a lasting change in the division of partisan strength in the electorate. If, on the other hand, the administration in power is *not* perceived as successful in handling the crisis, then in all likelihood the voters will reject that party in the next election, and its landslide victory in the previous election will be regarded, in retrospect, as a deviating election.

In a realignment it is very likely that the people who actually become partisans of the new majority party are the independents and previously uninvolved members of the electorate, not partisans of the other party. In other words, it seems that few Democrats or Republicans switch parties in a realignment but rather independents drop their independent stance and become partisans. Thus for a realignment to occur, a precondition may be a pool of people without partisan attachments who are "available" for realignment. This, in turn, suggests that there may be a longer sequence of events that form a realignment cycle.

First there is the crisis which, if successfully handled, leads to a realignment. This initiates a period of electoral stability during which the parties take distinct stands on the issues that were at the heart of the crisis. Party loyalty is high during this period, both within the electorate and among the elected political leaders in government. However, as time passes, new problems arise and new issues gradually disrupt the old alignment and lead to greater electoral instability. During this period, often referred to as a *dealignment*, voters are much more susceptible to the personal appeals of candidates, to local issues, and to other elements that might lead to departures from underlying party loyalty. As the time since the last realignment lengthens, more and more new voters come into the electorate without the attachments to the symbols and issues of the past that made their elders party loyalists. This group of voters without strong attachments to either party then may provide the basis for a new realignment should a crisis arise and one or the other of the parties be perceived as successfully solving it.

Party Systems and Major Realignments in American History

Political historians often divide American electoral history into five "party systems," eras that differed from each other in the different political parties that existed or in the different competitive relationships among the parties.[4] The transition from one party system to another has usually been marked by the occurrence of a realignment. The first party system, which extended from the 1790s until about 1824, saw the relatively rapid formation of two parties, the Federalists and the Jeffersonian Republicans. The issue that divided these parties most clearly was their attitude toward the power of the central government. The commercial and financial interests supported the Federalist position of increasing the authority of the central government whereas Jeffersonian Republicans distrusted the centralizing and, in their view, aristocratic tendencies of their rivals. These parties began as factions within the Congress but before long had gained organizations at the state and local level and had substantially broadened the base of political participation among the voting population. After 1815, competition between the two parties all but ceased as the Republicans gained supremacy, moving the country into the so-called "era of good feelings."

The second party system is usually dated from 1828, the year of the first presidential election with substantial popular participation, which marked the resurgence of party competition for the presidency. Emerging ultimately from this renewed competition were the Democrats and the Whigs, parties which competed fairly evenly for national power until the 1850s. Mass political participation increased and party organizations were strengthened as both parties sought electoral support from the common people. Although the Democratic party had come to prominence led by the westerner Jackson, by the 1850s both Democrats and Whigs had adherents in all sections of the nation. Thus when the issue of slavery broke full force upon the nation, the existing parties could not easily cope with the sectional differences they found within their ranks. As the Whigs and Democrats compromised or failed to act because of internal disagreements, a flurry of third parties appeared to push the cause of abolitionism. One of these, the Republican party, eventually replaced the floundering Whigs as one of the two major parties that would dominate party systems thereafter.

The intense conflicts preceding the Civil War led to the basic regional alignment of Democratic dominance in the South and Republi-

---

[4]See, for example, William N. Chambers and W. Dean Burnham (eds.), *The American Party Systems: Stages of Political Development* (New York: Oxford University Press, 1975).

can strength in the North that emerged from the war and that characterized the third party system. But the extreme intensity and durability of these partisan loyalties were also significantly dependent on emotional attachments associated with the war. The strength of these partisan attachments after the Civil War was not lessened by the sharp competitiveness of the two parties throughout the system. Electoral forces were so evenly balanced that the Republican party could control the presidency and Congress effectively only by excluding the southern Democrats from participation in elections. Once reconstruction relaxed enough to permit the full expression of Democratic strength, the nation was very narrowly divided, with the slightest deviation determining the outcome of elections.

The most dominant characteristic of the Civil War realignment was the regional division of party strongholds, but there was considerable Republican vote strength throughout much of the South and Democratic strength in most of the North. Especially in the North, states that regularly cast their electoral votes for Republican presidential candidates did so by very slim margins. Within each region persistent loyalty to the minority party was usually related to earlier opposition to the war. Seemingly, the intensity of feelings surrounding the war overwhelmed other issues, and the severity of the division over the war greatly inhibited the emergence of new issues along other lines. Thus a significant feature of the Civil War realignment is its "freezing" of the party system.[5] Although later realignments have occurred and, indeed, a fourth and fifth party system can be identified, after the Civil War the same two parties have remained dominant. The subsequent realignments only change the competitive position of these two parties relative to each other; the choices were "frozen" following the Civil War, although the relative strength of the parties was not. New parties find it impossible to compete effectively (though they may affect electoral outcomes), and the remnants of the sectional realignment of the Civil War are still visible and occasionally potent in the political conflicts of today.

Notice, too, that it was not until after the Civil War that a stable two-party system existed. The first party system became a one-party system dominated by the Jeffersonian Republican-Democrats, whereas the second party system became a highly fluid multiparty system.

---

[5]This concept was developed by S. M. Lipset and Stein Rokkan in their discussion of the development of European party systems in *Party Systems and Voter Alignments* (New York: The Free Press, 1967), pp. 1–64.

Toward the end of the nineteenth century, the Civil War loyalties weakened enough for third parties, particularly the Populists in the Midwest and South, to make inroads into the votes of both major parties. Following the economic recession of 1893 for which the Democrats suffered politically, the Republican party began to improve its basic vote strength. In 1896, the coalition of Democrats and Populists and the presidential candidacy of William Jennings Bryan resulted in increased Republican strength in the East, and the secure position of the Democratic party in the South became even stronger. Republican domination was further solidified in the Midwest by the popularity of Theodore Roosevelt in the election of 1904. By the early twentieth century, competitive areas were confined to the Border states and a few Mountain states.

It is appropriate to view the realignment of 1896 and the fourth party system that followed as an adjustment of the Civil War alignment. Few areas shifted very far from the previous levels of voting; probably most individuals did not change their partisanship. The issue basis of this alignment that differed from the Civil War divisions was economic, with the Republicans advocating development and modernization while opposing regulation of economic activity. The Democrats supported various policies intended to provide remedies for particular economic hardships. At a minimum these issues led the more prosperous, more modern areas in the North to shift toward the Republicans, and the more backward, more depressed areas of the South to shift toward the Democrats. These tendencies are based on normal vote patterns and should not obscure the considerable variation in the vote for president during these years, particularly in the elections of 1912 and 1916.

Following the depression of 1929, the Democrats emerged as the majority party, signaling the start of the fifth party system. The New Deal realignment resulted in far greater shifts than the prior realignment of 1896, since it shifted many of the northern states from Republican to Democratic status. The New Deal realignment has more present-day interest than the others, since it is the most recent and is reflected most prominently in present voting patterns. Since the policies of the Democratic administration during the New Deal appealed more to the working class than to the middle class, more to poor farmers than to the prosperous, these groups responded differently to Democratic candidates. The New Deal and the electorate's response to Roosevelt's administration considerably sharpened the social class basis of party support. Especially for younger voters during these years, class politics was of greater salience than it was before or has been since.

This resulted in adjustments in previous loyalties, but did not override them completely. The New Deal coalition was based on regional strength in the South, which was independent of social class, and further reinforced an already overwhelming dominance there. Perhaps the most incompatible elements in the New Deal coalition were the southern middle-class whites, mainly conservative, and the nothern liberals, both white and black.

Although the New Deal era established the basic pattern of partisanship leading to the present alignment, changes have occurred in several major components of this pattern of party loyalties. Most notably, southern whites have drifted away from the Democratic party, particularly in presidential contests. To a degree, working-class whites in the North also have moved toward the Republican party on occasion, and middle-class voters have sometimes shifted toward the Democrats. Figure 4-1 shows a considerable shift in the expected presidential votes of both the Republican and Democratic parties in the late 1960s.

The disintegration of the New Deal coalition should not be exaggerated, even though there has been erratic voting behavior in recent years. Deviations from Democratic loyalty have been most noticeable in presidential voting; the New Deal partisan alignment established in the 1930s remained intact longer in congressional voting. However, by the 1970s, further shifts in the New Deal alignment became evident, as conservative Republicans began to show strength in races for other offices in many parts of the South. Figure 4-2 presents the Democratic vote for Congress in the North and South since 1936 and illustrates the important role played by the South in Democratic victories through these years. The elections of the 1970s show the Democratic advantage in the South eroding; more and more Republicans are winning seats for the first time in many years. It probably is no exaggeration to suggest that in the South only long-standing Democratic incumbents are safe from competition, and as they step down, their seats will be contested by the Republicans. On the other hand, in some areas of the North moderate Republicans were replaced by liberal Democrats, reflecting weakness in long-established Republican support. The past several elections have revealed a degree of volatility in voting that suggests detachment from the partisan sympathies associated with the New Deal alignment.

Following the 1980 election, there was prompt speculation that a realignment was underway. The obvious indication of Republican re-

FIGURE 4-2 Democratic Vote for Congress, North and South, 1936–1984

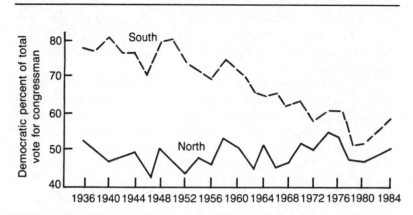

Source: U.S. Bureau of the Census, *Statistical Abstract of the United States, 1986,* 106th ed. (Washington D.C.: U.S. Government Printing Office, 1985).

surgence was Reagan's victory over Carter by 10 percent of the popular vote, his lopsided victory in the electoral college, and Republican control of the Senate for the first time since 1954. Modest increases in Republican party identification associated with the election of 1980, monitored by various news organizations, proved to be shortlived. By the election of 1982, in the midst of an economic recession and a period of high unemployment, a resurgence of Democratic strength had occurred and potential Democratic nominee Walter Mondale led President Reagan comfortably in the polls through much of 1983. Political analysts were characterizing this as a Republican collapse, another abortive realignment occasioned by the apparent failure of Reagan's economic policies. But as the economy rallied and the Democratic internecine primary battles took their toll, President Reagan scored an impressive landslide victory in 1984, immediately refueling talk of Republican realignment.

The evidence on this point is inconclusive. The best academic data collected during the 1984 campaign and presented as parts of Tables 2–1 and 2–2 show no particular gains in party identification. In the year after the 1984 election there was some fluctuation in party strength but basically the two parties were in roughly the same position at the end of 1985 as at the start, according to the surveys done by the Gallup Poll.[6] If anything has changed in party identification recently, it is a slight decline in independence. There is very little indication that the Republicans are gaining at the expense of the Democrats. Thus rather clear changes in voting behavior—at least at the presidential level—have not been accompanied by clear changes in party identification.

Unlike realignments in the past for which analysis has been limited due to the absence of survey data, we have the opportunity during the current period to study the individual processes of partisan change that underlie the changes in the aggregate shifts in the partisan division of the electorate. These processes have been a matter of some controversy. One perspective holds that individual partisans are converted from one party to the other during a realignment. Other analysts, noting the psychological difficulty in changing long-held and deeply felt attachments, argue that such change probably comes about through "mobilization" rather than conversion. In other words, it is the independents or nonpolitical individuals, perhaps predominantly young voters just entering the electorate without strong partisan attachments, who fuel a realignment by joining the electorate overwhelmingly on the side of one party.

Some evidence on these points comes from the New Deal era. Although survey research was then in its infancy, some scholars have creatively used data from early surveys to try to answer these questions. Research by Kristi Andersen, reported in *The Changing American Voter*,[7] reveals high levels of nonvoting and nonpartisanship among young people and new citizens prior to the depression. Those uninvolved, uncommitted potential participants entered the electorate in the 1930s disproportionately as Democrats. Andersen's findings on the electorate of the 1920s and 1930s support the view that realignments are based on the mobilization of new, independent voters rather than on the conversion of partisans. In contrast, Erikson and Tedin argue on the basis of early Gallup Poll data that much of

---

[6]The Gallup Poll estimates of Republican party identification are consistently higher than those of the Center for Political Studies used throughout this book. Both surveys use in-person interviewing rather than telephoning. However, the Gallup organization does its polling very rapidly, usually in three days, and cannot devote the time and resources to tracking down respondents that the Center for Political Studies can. This appears to yield a larger percentage of Republicans, and probably a sample with higher social status, for Gallup than for the Center for Political Studies.

[7]Norman H. Nie, Sidney Verba, and John R. Petrocik, *The Changing American Voter* (Cambridge, Mass.: Harvard University Press, 1976), chap. 5.

the increase in the Democratic vote in the 1930s came from voters who had previously voted Republican.[8]

In the next section we will examine these processes of partisan change in the contemporary period. Although we are in a better position to do so than for earlier eras, efforts are still hampered by a scarcity of panel data, that is, repeated interviews with the same individuals at different points in time. Most of the time, it will be necessary to infer individual changes from the behavior of similar types of individuals at different times.

Partisan Change

Two types of change in partisan identification can be distinguished, both of which have significant implications for political behavior. First, an individual may change from one party to another or to independent, or from independence to partisanship. Such change is of obvious importance if a large proportion of the electorate shift in the same direction at about the same time. Second, an individual's partisanship may strengthen or weaken in intensity. A long-standing hypothesis states that the longer individuals identify with a party the stronger their partisanship will become.[9] In the electorate as a whole, these two types of change are not necessarily related to one another, so the occurrence of one form of change does not dictate or prevent the other. The existing increase in numbers of independents at the expense of Democrats and Republicans does not necessarily mean that among the remaining partisans there has been no strengthening of loyalty with the lengthening of identification.

Analysts have attempted to explain partisan change by referring to three types of causal effects: (1) period effects, or the impact of a particular historical period that briefly affects partisanship across all age groups; (2) a generation effect, which affects the partisanship of a particular age group for the remainder of their political lives; and (3) a life-cycle effect, which produces changes associated with an individual's age. In current political behavior all three can be illustrated. There is a period effect that has resulted in an increasing indepen-

---

[8]Robert S. Erikson and Kent L. Tedin, "The 1928–1936 Partisan Realignment: The Case for the Conversion Hypothesis," *American Political Science Review* 75 (December 1981): 951–962.

[9]Philip E. Converse, *The Dynamics of Party Support: Cohort-Analyzing Party Identification* (Beverly Hills, Calif.: Sage Publications, 1976).

dence in all age groups, a generation effect that keeps Democratic partisan loyalty high in the generation that entered the electorate during the New Deal, and a life-cycle effect that yields greater independence among the young than among their elders.

The differences between the 1950s and 1970s in the proportion of independents in various age groups is shown in Figure 4–3. The solid line represents the percentage of independents in each age group in 1984 and the dotted line represents 1974. These two lines reflect the much higher rate of independence among the young in the recent years compared with 1952, the broken line. The older age groups in 1974, and in 1984 those over sixty, are about the same as voters of comparable age were in 1952. However, in 1952 there were only slight differences associated with age, evidenced by the flatness of the broken line in Figure 4–3. The youngest individuals were only a little more likely to be independent than the elderly and not nearly so likely to be independent as young people twenty years later.

It is also possible to examine the change in particular age "cohorts" between 1952 and the later years using Figure 4–3.[10] The youngest cohort in 1952 was forty to forty-six years old in 1974 and reveals a substantially higher level of independence than it did when entering the electorate. By 1984, this cohort was fifty to fifty-six years old and had become less independent once again. At each point along the lines, the vertical distance represents the changing percentage of independents in that age cohort. Most age cohorts became more independent during the early 1970s and have become somewhat less independent recently. For the most part, though, cohorts are more independent than they were in the 1950s.

Contrary to political folklore, there is little evidence that people become Republicans as they grow older, that is, that a life-cycle effect favors Republicans. On the other hand, it is true that older members

---

[10]In the absence of repeated observations of the same individuals over time, it is impossible to study many aspects of change. The use of age cohorts is an analytic technique that attempts to assess individual change through the use of surveys of different individuals over the years. Individuals of a certain age are isolated in an early survey, say, thirty- to forty-year-olds in 1956, and they are compared with forty- to fifty-year-olds from a 1966 survey. This makes possible the comparison of an "age cohort" at two different times. This technique has been used in several studies of partisanship. See, for example, Paul R. Abramson, "Generational Change in American Electoral Behavior," *American Political Science Review* 68 (March 1974): 93–105; David Butler and Donald Stokes, *Political Change in Britain: Forces Shaping Electoral Choice* (New York: St. Martin's Press, 1969), esp. chaps. 3, 11; and Converse, *The Dynamics of Party Support.*

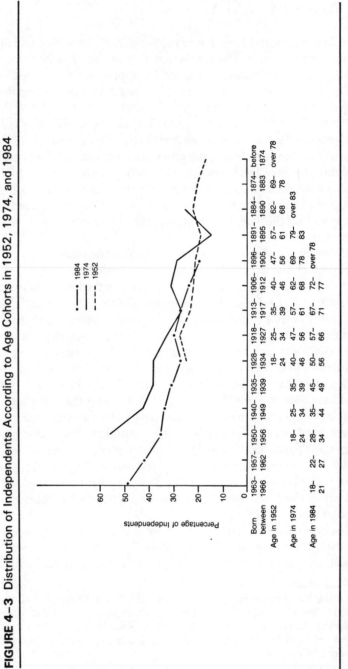

FIGURE 4–3 Distribution of Independents According to Age Cohorts in 1952, 1974, and 1984

Source: Recalculated from Warren E. Miller and Teresa E. Levitin, *Leadership and Change* (Cambridge, Mass.; Winthrop Publishers, 1976), p. 246; Center for Political Studies 1984 National Election Study.

of the electorate were, for some years, more likely to be Republicans than younger members. The generation of young people who came of age prior to the depression contained large proportions of Republicans, an understandable situation given the advantage the Republicans enjoyed nationally at that time. Relatively few members of this generation have changed partisanship over the years, and these individuals constituted the older, more heavily Republican segment of the electorate. By the same token, the generation that entered the electorate during the New Deal was disproportionately Democratic. Since they also have remained stable in partisanship, older voters now look increasingly Democratic as this generation ages. For a decade or so it will appear that the older the voters are, the more likely they are to be Democratic.

The tendency of individual partisanship to strengthen with age is the subject of some controversy.[11] During periods of stable party voting there is likely to be increased partisanship the longer individuals identify with and vote for their party. On the other hand, when party voting is frequently disrupted, this reinforcement of partisanship may not occur. Even when the strength of partisanship does not increase with age, as appears to be the case in recent years, older partisans are less likely to abandon their party for an independent stance.

Gradual changes in individual partisanship have not been assessed satisfactorily for the entire public because the few election studies with repeated interviews of the same individuals have covered at most four years. Nevertheless, the possibility that individuals change their partisanship over longer time periods is of considerable interest. In recent years speculation has focused on the possibility that the large number of young independents will become identified with one party or the other, thus creating a substantial shift in the overall partisan balance of the electorate.

The best evidence on this point comes from a major study of political socialization, conducted by M. Kent Jennings.[12] He surveyed a national sample of high school students and their parents in 1965,

---

[11]The main participants in this controversy are Philip Converse and Paul Abramson. See Converse's *The Dynamics of Party Support*, and Abramson's "Developing Party Identification: A Further Examination of Life-Cycle, Generational, and Period Effects," *American Journal of Political Science* 23 (February 1979): 78–96.

[12]The major findings of the first two waves of this study have been reported in M. Kent Jennings and Richard G. Niemi, *The Political Character of Adolescence: The Influence of Families and Schools* (Princeton, N.J.: Princeton University Press, 1974), and *Generation and Politics* (Princeton, N.J.: Princeton University Press,

with follow-up interviews in 1973 and 1982. This provides a before-and-after picture of young people during the political traumas of the late 1960s and early 1970s, as well as a later snapshot after a more quiescent period. The interviews with the parents allow comparison with an older group experiencing the same political events.

As can be seen in Table 4–1, the parental group was highly stable in their partisanship, with only 3 or 4 percent switching from one party to the other and approximately three-fourths maintaining their party identification from one interview to the next. About one in five switched into or out of the independent category. Between each time period, about equal numbers switched in each direction so the aggregate or net change was nonexistent for the parents.

TABLE 4–1 Stability and Change of Partisanship in Two Cohorts, High School Seniors in 1965 and Their Parents

		Young People							
		1973					*1982*		
		Dem	Ind	Rep			Dem	Ind	Rep
	Dem	24	14	3		Dem	23	9	3
1965	Ind	7	24	5	1973	Ind	8	32	7
	Rep	3	9	10		Rep	2	4	13
		Total = 99%	n = 952				Total = 101%	n = 924	

		Parents							
		1973					*1982*		
		Dem	Ind	Rep			Dem	Ind	Rep
	Dem	39	5	3		Dem	37	6	2
1965	Ind	5	16	5	1973	Ind	6	16	3
	Rep	1	4	23		Rep	2	4	24
		Total = 101%	n = 838				Total = 100%	n = 822	

Source: Recalculated from M. Kent Jennings and Gregory B. Markus, "Partisan Orientation over the Long Haul," *American Political Science Review* 78, no. 4 (December 1984): pp. 1004–5, tables 2 and 3.

1981); a report on partisanship using all three waves of interviews is contained in M. Kent Jennings and Gregory B. Markus, "Partisan Orientation Over the Long Haul: Results from the Three Wave Political Socialization Panel Study," *American Political Science Review* 78 (December 1984): 1000–1018.

The young people were less stable in their partisanship, especially between 1965 and 1973 when both Democratic and Republican identifiers among the young shifted in large numbers to an independent status. During the next interval from 1973 to 1982, these same young people were more stable in their loyalties, with about two-thirds maintaining the same party identification. This group, which was roughly thirty-four years old in 1982, remained much more independent than their parents but the numbers of independents among them had not increased over this decade. As with their parents, very few young people (about one in twenty) switched from party to party during either time period.

The change in the partisan composition of the electorate through generational change is ordinarily a very gradual one, since political attitudes, including partisanship, tend to be transmitted from parents to their children. Normally, more than two-thirds of the electorate identify with their parents' party if both parents had the same party identification. Certainly the adoption of parents' partisanship by their children is consistent with the notion of family socialization. Children pick up the partisanship of their parents while quite young, but the parents' influence lessens as the child comes into contact with other political and social influences in the teenage years. Of course, for most individuals the political influence of their surroundings will be consistent with their family's political leanings, so the similarity between parents' and offspring's partisanship remains strong. On the other hand, people who remember their parents as having conflicting loyalties are more likely to be independents than either Democrats or Republicans. This is even more true of the children of parents without any partisan attachments. Thus in each political generation a sizable number of voters lacks an inherited party loyalty.

The Jennings study also permits the examination of the process of generational change since it allows a comparison of party identification for parents and their children. As can be seen in Figure 4-4a, 58 percent of the seventeen-year-olds in 1965 had adopted the party identification of their parents. Of the high school seniors, 30 percent were Democratic and came from Democratic families. Democrats had a somewhat higher "transmission rate" than either Republicans or independents. Despite this higher transmission rate, there were so many more Democratic parents that their children also contributed substantial numbers to the independent ranks.

As we saw before, the parents changed very little between 1965 and 1973, whereas the young people became markedly more independent. Thus by the later date, fewer than half of the children share

FIGURE 4–4a Party Identification of High School Seniors and Their Parents in 1965

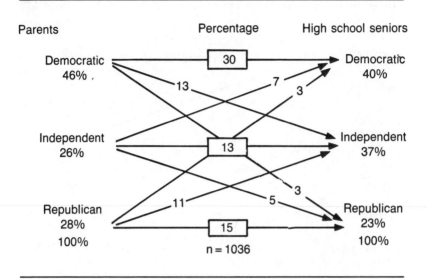

Parents   Percentage   High school seniors

Democratic 46%   30   Democratic 40%

Independent 26%   13   Independent 37%

Republican 28%   15   Republican 23%

100%   n = 1036   100%

Note on reading figure: On the left is the distribution of the parents' party identification and on the right is their children's. The numbers in the three boxes highlight the percentages of the children who had the same party identification as their parents. The numbers on the remaining arrows show various amounts of change from their parents' partisanship by the children. For example, 7 percent of the total number of children had independent parents but became Democrats.

Source: Recomputed from Paul A. Beck, Jere W. Bruner, and L. Douglas Dobson, *Political Socialization* (Washington, D.C.: American Political Science Association, 1974), p. 22.

their parents' party identification. As we can see in Figure 4–4*b*, by 1973, only half the children of Democratic parents were also Democrats and only a little over one-third of the Republican offspring were still Republicans. The increasing strength of independents drew from both parties about equally. Between 1973 and 1982, there was no further erosion of the children's loyalty away from their parents' party. If anything, these young people drifted back to the party identification of their childhood.

These data from the Jennings study continue to show substantial transmission of parental political views, although not the high level of durability that earlier findings had suggested. It is reasonable to sup-

FIGURE 4–4b Party Identification of Twenty-Five-Year-Olds in 1973 and Their Parents in 1965

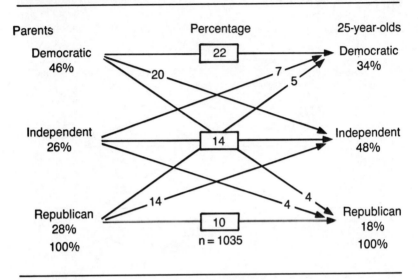

Source: Calculated from data provided with Paul A. Beck, Jere W. Bruner, and L. Douglas Dobson, *Political Socialization* (Washington, D.C.: American Political Science Association, 1974).

pose that in more quiet times there would be greater continuity in the political views of parents and children.

This discussion of partisan change has relevance for understanding the process of electoral realignment. It suggests that changes in the party loyalty of the electorate observed during realignment are less the result of individuals changing from one party to another than of new voters, both young people and the previously uninvolved, who come into the electorate with a different distribution of party loyalties than did previous generations. A critical question is the extent to which the youngest members of the electorate, large numbers of whom were independent during the 1970s, are now abandoning independence and adopting a Republican partisanship in response to the policies and perceived successes of the Reagan administration.

Figures 4–5a and b present a cohort analysis of the electorate, focusing on the changing percentages of Republicans and Democrats in 1976, 1980, and 1984. This figure is read in similar fashion to Figure 4–3, which examined the changing percentage of independents. The vertical distances between the lines on the graph represent the amount

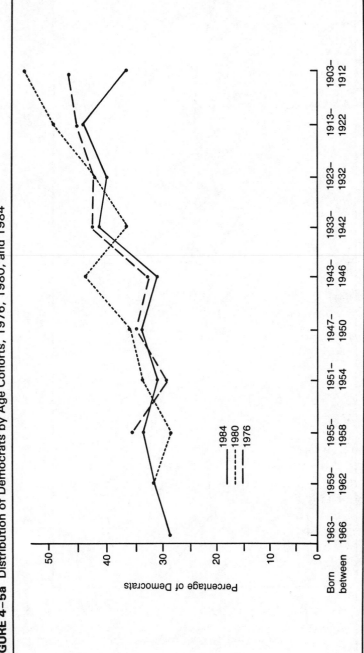

FIGURE 4–5a Distribution of Democrats by Age Cohorts, 1976, 1980, and 1984

89

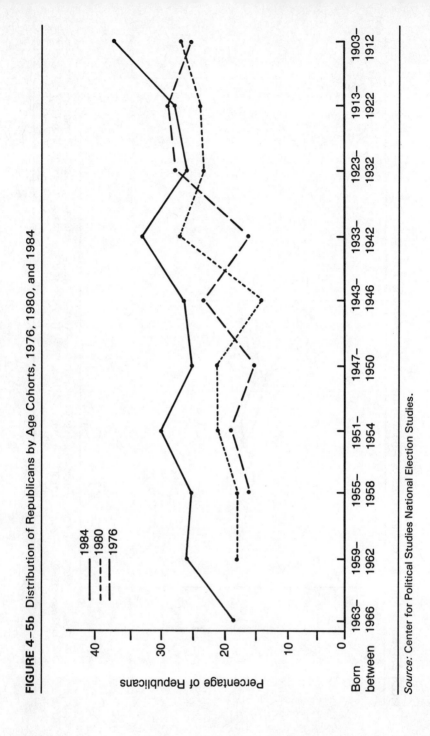

FIGURE 4–5b Distribution of Republicans by Age Cohorts, 1976, 1980, and 1984

Source: Center for Political Studies National Election Studies.

of change in each cohort over these years. As can be seen in Figure 4–5*b*, Republican percentages have increased in the young and middle-age cohorts since 1976, with most of the increase coming since 1980, at least in the younger cohorts. This shift has been entirely at the expense of independents; Democratic strength, as shown in Figure 4–5*a*, has not eroded in any of these cohorts since 1976. The Democrats have maintained their advantage over the Republicans in the face of this movement because each cohort has entered the electorate considerably more Democratic than Republican. This Democratic advantage continued in 1984 among eighteen- to twenty-one-year-olds even while the slightly older members of the electorate were moving toward the Republican Party.

What, then, does this mean for the question of a Reagan realignment? The best evidence suggests that there has been some net increase in Republican party identification since the late 1970s. This increase has amounted to about five percent and has been rather irregular (1982 represented a setback for the Republicans, for example). Over time, of course, these gradual increases among the youngest members of the electorate could constitute a significant shift that would substantially alter the partisan balance in the electorate. The key will be the extent to which this gradual increase among the young will be sustained after Reagan passes from the electoral scene in 1988. At the very least, we can expect a continued Republican competitiveness in contests for the presidency and a narrower margin of difference between the parties in the number of their identifiers.

5

Public Opinion
and Ideology

$$\star\,\star\,\star$$

The collective attitudes of the public, or of segments of the public, toward the issues of the day is another significant aspect of American political behavior. The study of public opinion is of obvious relevance to public officials and political journalists who wish to assess the mood of the people on various topics, but the extent to which decision makers are influenced by public opinion on any particular policy is almost impossible to determine. Although there must be some sense of the public mood as policy is being made, no one supposes that policy makers measure precisely the attitudes of the public or are influenced by public opinion alone.

An additional concern is political ideology, a set of interrelated attitudes that fit together into some coherent and consistent view of or orientation toward the political world. Political ideologies in the contemporary United States normally are described in terms of liberalism or conservatism, but other dimensions are possible. This chapter will present an examination of opinions on several major public issues and then turn to a consideration of the ideological perspectives of the American public. In the next chapter, major attention will be directed to the impact of issue concerns on individual voting decisions.

Public Opinion on Political Issues

In American society public attitudes toward policies usually can be described in one of two ways: as *permissive* opinion—that is, that a wide range of government activity is acceptable to the public—and, in contrast, as *directive* opinion, either supportive or negative, that specifies certain alternatives that are definitely demanded or opposed. Ordinarily, policy alternatives advocated by both political parties are within the range of permissive opinion, a situation that does not create highly salient issues nor sharp cleavages in the public even though political leaders may present their various positions dramatically. Only if many people hold directive opinions will the level of issue salience rise or issue clashes appear among the public. For example, undoubtedly there is widespread directive support for public education in this country; most individuals demand a system for public education or would demand it were it threatened. At the same time there is permissive support for a wide range of policies and programs in public education. Governments at several levels may engage in a variety of programs without arousing the public to opposition or support. Within this permissive range the public is indifferent.

On occasion, out-and-out opposition to programs develops, and directive opinion is formed that imposes a limit on how far government can go. For example, the widespread opposition to busing children out of their neighborhoods for purposes of integration has perhaps become a directive, negative opinion. It is no easy matter for political analysts or politicians to discover the boundaries between permissive and directive opinions, and political leaders are likely to argue that there are supportive, directive opinions for their own positions and negative, directive opinions for the views of their opponents. One should be skeptical of these claims because it is much more likely that there are permissive opinions and casual indifference toward the alternative views. Indifference is widespread and of course does not create political pressure. Rather, it frees political leaders of restrictions on issue positions but, on balance, is probably more frustrating than welcome.

The commercial opinion-polling organizations have spent fifty years asking Americans about their views on matters of public policy. Most of this investigation has taken either of two forms: (1) asking individuals whether they "approve or disapprove of" or "agree or disagree with" a statement of policy, and (2) asking individuals to pick their preference among two or more alternative statements of policy. This form of questioning seriously exaggerates the number of people who hold views on political issues. People can easily say "agree" or "disapprove" in response to a question, even if they know nothing at all about the topic. If given the opportunity, many people will volunteer the information that they hold no views on specific items of public policy. In 1964, for example, more than one-third of the American electorate had no opinion on United States involvement in Vietnam. In contrast, on the issue of abortion in 1980 fewer than 5 percent of all adults were without an opinion. More typically, in recent years around 10 percent of the electorate has had no opinion on major issues of public policy. Another 10 to 20 percent are unaware of what the government is doing in a policy area or where the parties and candidates stand on an issue. Beyond these two categories of relatively uninformed individuals, Philip Converse has shown that a number of those individuals who appear to have an opinion may be regarded as responding to policy questions at random.[1]

There are a number of ways of explaining this lack of opinion and information on topics of public policy. Generally, the same factors that explain nonvoting account for the absence of opinions. Individuals with little interest in or concern with politics are least likely to have opinions on matters of public policy. Beyond this basic relationship, low socioeconomic status is associated with no opinion on issues; low income and little education create social circumstances in which individuals are less likely to have views and information on public policies.

It is no simple matter to describe the distribution of opinions in the American electorate because no obvious, widely accepted way has been established to measure these opinions. Or, to put it another way, asking different questions in public opinion polls will elicit different answers. The distribution of opinions on, say, abortion could be substantially altered by asking respondents whether they approve of "killing unborn children" as opposed to "letting women have control over their own bodies." Furthermore, there is no direct means to validate measures of opinions as there is with reports of voting behavior. Consequently, descriptions of public opinion must be taken as more uncertain, more tentative than conclusions drawn from the discussion of partisanship because independent indicators of opinions on public issues are rare.

---

[1]Philip Converse, "The Nature of Belief Systems in Mass Publics," *Ideology and Discontent*, ed. David Apter (New York: The Free Press of Glencoe, 1964), pp. 238–245.

Political analysts and public officials both have difficulty assessing the likely impact of public opinion as measured by public opinion polls because the intensity of feelings will influence the willingness of the public to act on their views. Public officials who value their careers must be more conscious of the issues that raise feelings intense enough to cause people to contribute money, campaign, and cast their ballots solely on the basis of that issue. As a result, public officials may be more responsive to the desires of small, intense groups than to larger, but basically indifferent, segments of the public.

Issue Positions and Partisanship

There are many dimensions of opinion on public policy: economic affairs, race relations, international affairs, and a variety of moral, social, and cultural concerns. To be sure, these issue areas have many facets and only a few themes dominate public attention at any one time. Not only does public attention to particular issues rise and fall, but the pattern of interrelationships among different sets of issues also changes over time.

Analysts of American political history draw special attention to those rare periods when a single issue dimension dominates the public's views of governmental policy. Periods like the Civil War or the New Deal revealed deep, salient divisions in the public, paralleled by a distinctiveness in the issue stands of the political parties. Electoral realignments of voters are forged by these unusually strong issue alignments, and during such times we would expect a close correspondence between attitudes on the relevant issues and partisanship.

At other times, highly salient issues may capture the attention of the public, but they are likely to cut across, rather than reinforce, other issue positions and party loyalties. If the parties do not take clearly differentiated stands on such issues and if party supporters are divided in their feelings toward the issues, party loyalty and the existing partisan alignment are undermined. In a complex political system like the United States, new, dissimilar issue divisions accumulate until a crisis causes one dimension to dominate and obscure other issues.

The New Deal alignment, which underlies the present partisan division, was based primarily on domestic economic issues. These issues continue to be the ones on which the political parties take the most distinctive stands. Otherwise, there has been considerable disarray in recent years among a number of salient issues; some of these are long-standing, like race; others are new, like abortion and energy policy. The Reagan administration's efforts to reduce the federal government's role in providing social services has the potential to restore much of the New Deal alignment around a cleavage of domestic economic issues.

The following is an analysis of several issue areas, of their interrelationships, and of the relationship of social characteristics and partisanship to opinions on issues. A leading assumption is that partisan identification provides guidance for the public on policy matters—that is, most Americans hold their opinions by following what they perceive to be the view consistent with their partisanship. Of course, it also is likely that policy positions developed independently of one's partisanship but consistent with it will reinforce feelings of party loyalty or that attitudes on issues will lead to a preference for the party most in agreement with them. Furthermore, issue preferences inconsistent with party loyalty can erode or change it. For any particular individual it would be extremely difficult to untangle the effects of partisanship and policy preferences over a long period of time. Common sense suggests that many other elements of personality and circumstances contribute to the development of issue positions, so it is no surprise to find many political views existing quite independently of partisanship.

The relationship between attitudes on public policy and partisanship is not particularly strong in any event. Even though on many issues most partisans of one party will certainly have a position different from that held by the majority of the other party, large numbers of people with issue positions "inconsistent" with their party identification remain. To account for this, it is variously suggested that: (1) issues are unimportant to many voters; (2) only the issues most salient to individuals need be congruent with their partisanship; (3) individuals regularly misperceive the positions of the parties in order to remain comfortable with both their party loyalty and their policy preferences; or (4) the positions of each party are so ambiguous or so dissimilar in different areas of the country that no clear distinction exists between the parties and thus it is not surprising that partisans of different parties appear so similar. Undoubtedly, all of these explanations have some degree of truth. A long time has elapsed since there has been a crisis that would realign issues along party lines, so it is understandable that a great many issues are relatively independent of partisan ties. Only on traditional domestic economic issues, which have formed the basic ideological division between the parties since the New Deal, are the differences among the issue positions of partisans at all dramatic.

There is some evidence that the relationship between partisanship and issue positions has strengthened in recent years. Gerald Pomper[2] examined Survey Research Center data from 1956 to 1972. Using as his data the answers to a comparable set of questions on public policies, he found that Republicans and Democrats had become more polarized on issues and perceptions of parties. Comparable questions asked after 1972 reveal consistent, if not strong, relationships between partisanship and issue stands.

One bit of folklore about American politics has been that economic issues are more important to the voter than other issues. Domestic economic issues are frequently treated by politicians and political analysts as the real forces at work in the political system, sometimes openly and sometimes hidden behind a facade of other issues. This view has a certain plausibility. Indeed there have been periods when economic issues were paramount, but there is no reason to assume that any one type of issue will always be more important than others.

Over the past decade, the public's view of the relative importance of domestic and foreign policy matters has varied considerably. Foreign policy problems did not appear prominent between the end of the Korean War and the beginning of heavy United States involvement in Vietnam. In that interim, domestic economic matters dominated the public's view of the nation's problems. In the 1960s, race-related problems were mentioned increasingly, with concern over urban unrest added to various aspects of segregation and integration. By the late 1960s, Vietnam was the single most important problem mentioned by Americans, although the entire set of domestic economic concerns outweighed that single foreign policy problem. In 1972, foreign affairs, Vietnam in particular, declined in salience but still remained the single most important concern. Since the early 1970s, economic problems have become more salient. Although Iran captured the public's attention dramatically from late 1979 to early 1981, concern over economic problems approached crisis proportions. In the 1980s, no problems other than the economy held the public's attention for any length of time.

---

[2]Gerald Pomper, *Voters' Choice: Varieties of American Electoral Behavior* (New York: Dodd, Mead & Co., 1975), chap. 8.

Domestic Economic Issues

Ronald Reagan's landslide victory in 1980 and his administration's subsequent efforts at dismantling the social programs enacted by administrations of both parties in previous decades has been portrayed as a reversal of fifty years of economic liberalism. In policy terms this may well be the case. It is not true, however, that such a policy shift reflects any change in the American public's persistent willingness to support federal governmental programs intended to solve social problems. In economic matters Americans are more liberal than conservative. Increased government activity in domestic economic affairs or in welfare programs elicits no widespread, consistent public opposition. In recent years the main source of public opposition to federal government activities appears to be based on opposition to racial integration and not based on economic considerations. To be sure, some individuals in the electorate oppose government economic activities for other reasons, but the ideological opponents of government activity are not numerous in the general public. In this respect, as in many others, the substantial number of political leaders, including President Reagan, who oppose "liberal" domestic economic programs is not a reflection of public opinion.

Figure 5–1 shows the distribution of attitudes toward spending for different governmental purposes. These data were collected by the General Social Survey from 1973 to 1983. There is considerable variation in the belief that too much is being spent on welfare, with low points in the mid-1970s and early 1980s. The pattern of attitudes on spending to protect the environment is more stable and more typical of attitudes toward other domestic economic policies. Very few comparable survey questions have been asked over the years about domestic issues—the issues come and go fairly rapidly—but the same pattern of stability would probably emerge from more extensive analysis.

When an examination of the relationship between social characteristics and issue stands on traditional economic issues (such as the choice between reducing spending and maintaining government services) is made, one can expect to find dramatic differences among social groups. The pattern in Figure 5–2 is not too difficult to describe: the least economically secure, blacks and poorly educated southern whites, support government services most strongly. The better educated are most opposed to government spending. Two groups do not fit this interpretation. The Jewish group, which is generally well educated and affluent, is quite supportive of government services, a char-

FIGURE 5-1 Attitudes toward Domestic Policies, 1973–1983

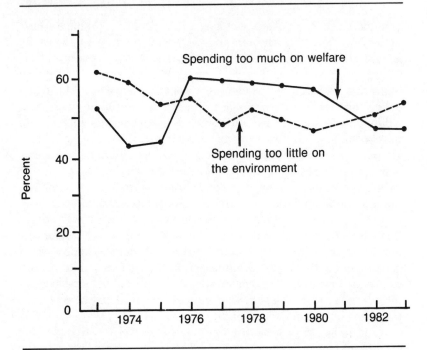

Source: NORC, *General Social Surveys, 1972–1982,* pp. 76, 79; *General Social Surveys, 1972–1983,* pp. 76, 79.

acteristic that has been true for many years. Among Catholics in the North, the grade school-educated are the least supportive of government services, but this finding may be a function of the small number of such respondents in the survey.

Favoring services over spending cuts represents the type of choice in governmental policy that characterized the New Deal. Thus it would be reasonable to expect a dramatic difference between Democrats and Republicans on such an issue. Economic issues have divided Democrats and Republicans since the 1930s. During these decades, partisans have supported or opposed economic issues quite consistently, whereas other issues have been only of temporary significance for the parties. Consequently, the relationship in Table 5–1 showing that Democrats are disproportionately in favor of maintaining government services to which Republicans tend to be opposed is no surprise. Strong Democrats favor maintaining government services over reducing spending by a margin of 68 percent to 15 percent,

FIGURE 5–2 Attitudes toward Cutting or Maintaining Government Services According to Region, Race, Religion, and Education, 1984

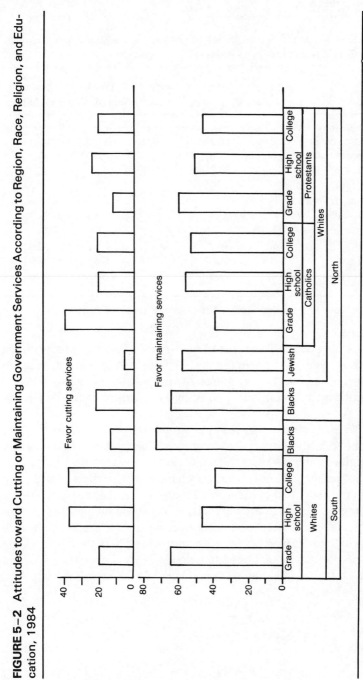

Source: Center for Political Studies 1984 National Election Study.

TABLE 5–1 Attitudes toward Spending Cuts versus Maintaining Government Services According to Partisanship, 1984

	Strong Democrats	Weak Democrats	Inde- pendents	Weak Republicans	Strong Republicans
Strongly favors spending cuts	7%	12%	14%	10%	23%
Moderate	8	9	13	14	17
Neutral	16	17	19	23	32
Moderate	16	20	18	23	12
Strongly favors maintaining government services	52	42	35	29	16
Total	99%	100%	99%	99%	100%
n =	260	288	535	230	198

Source: Center for Political Studies 1984 National Election Study.

while strong Republicans are just the opposite, favoring a reduction in spending over government services 40 percent to 28 percent. It is also important to observe that noticeable proportions of Democrats and Republicans hold opinions opposed by a majority of their fellow partisans.

Partisanship may not lead individuals to hold the views they do, but the stability of party loyalty makes it likely that views on policy are influenced by partisanship. Individuals abandon their party over an issue presumably only when they have exceptionally intense feeling about the issue. It should be noted that very few issues cause extreme or intense differences among social groups or among partisans. Neither social circumstances nor political parties seem to provide such clearcut, persuasive cues for most individuals that their own values and perceptions cannot operate independently. Political, social, and personal factors all diminish the dramatic differences that might exist on public issues.

Social and Racial Issues

The most persistently volatile issues in American history have dealt with problems surrounding the treatment of blacks. After many years of little public attention to this problem, integration became a major focus of national and international attention in the 1950s. Two significant developments in the distribution of attitudes have been associated with this issue. First, during the past twenty years southern blacks have become increasingly concerned with public policies affecting them and have changed from a largely apathetic, uninterested group to a concerned, involved, politically motivated group. Second, large numbers of southern whites have adjusted their opinions to accept the realities of the new legal and political position of blacks. White southerners have not come to prefer integrated schools, but many have been willing to accept them. Support for school integration is high among blacks in both the South and the North, and support is lower among whites. Among northern whites the greatest opposition to integration is found among groups living closest to black neighborhoods, except for farmers, who display consistently lower levels of support for integrated schools. Attitudes toward school integration are rather complex in the North, where whites are more supportive of integration than are white southerners but are overwhelmingly opposed to busing. When a national sample of high school seniors from 1965 were re-interviewed in 1973, a sharp erosion in support for school integration was found among the white, northern young people.[3] During the same period, southern whites changed relatively little but, if anything, became more supportive of integration.

Differences in support for school integration are associated with partisanship, although this results mainly from blacks being strongly in favor of integration and also overwhelmingly Democratic. Among whites in both the North and the South, patterns are neither strong nor consistent. In general, attitudes on integration are better explained by social and personal characteristics than by partisanship. In part, the reason for this may be that the leaders of both parties take similar stands on such issues in a given constituency; consequently the parties do not provide differing cues or leadership and in fact may simply be responding to a nearly universal sentiment in their districts. In other cases the leaders of one party may disagree among themselves on such issues, consequently keeping a party from offering consistent cues and leadership on these matters of public policy.

Another area of domestic policy that has received attention is the relation of governmental institutions to religious organizations, in

---

[3]These data are available from the Inter-university Consortium for Political and Social Research in a data set with Paul Allen Beck, Jere W. Bruner, and L. Douglas Dobson, *Political Socialization* (Washington, D.C.: American Political Science Association, 1974).

particular state support for parochial education and prayers in public schools. As with other areas of social and racial policy, the public is partially responding to Supreme Court decisions. Attitudes toward parochial school support are heavily influenced by an individual's perceived religious interests. Generally, Americans would prefer more mixing of church and state, not less. For example, over two-thirds of adults support the practice of starting public school classes with a prayer. Even though these attitudes have been consistent for twenty years, the issue of prayer in the schools has only recently become mobilized into a political force nationally. In contrast, the Supreme Court decision on abortion immediately generated a polarized response. The question of abortion taps a whole cluster of divisive issues, ranging from sectarian religious beliefs, to the redefinition of sex roles, to concern with overpopulation, to attitudes toward welfare mothers with occasional overtones of racism. As such, abortion is a volatile issue that in some areas has turned election races into one-issue campaigns.

The public's views on abortion are associated with several personal characteristics, most notably age, education, and religion. No matter what combination of characteristics are examined in the general public, invariably more than half of the people support the right to abortion under some circumstances.[4] In simple terms, generally young people favor the right to abortion, the elderly are much more likely to oppose it, the less well educated are less supportive of legal abortion than the better educated, and Catholics overall are more inclined than Protestants to oppose abortions.

When these three characteristics are examined jointly, each retains some influence on the distribution of opinions on abortion. Figure 5–3 shows the net "pro-choice" versus "pro-life" percentages. The percentage taking the most extreme pro-life position was subtracted from the percentage taking the most extreme pro-choice position. Thus a positive number in Figure 5–3 indicates a preponderance of

---

[4]These figures undoubtedly underestimate the proportion taking the "pro-life" position. The two response choices at the pro-life end of the continuum were: abortion should never be permitted and abortion should be permitted only to save the life or health of the mother. The first is a more extreme position than many pro-life advocates would take; on the other hand, the second includes circumstances (health reasons) that have been explicitly rejected by pro-life advocates in and out of Congress. Thus neither category is an entirely satisfactory indicator of pro-life sentiment. We have used the most extreme category at either end of the continuum to indicate pro-life and pro-choice positions.

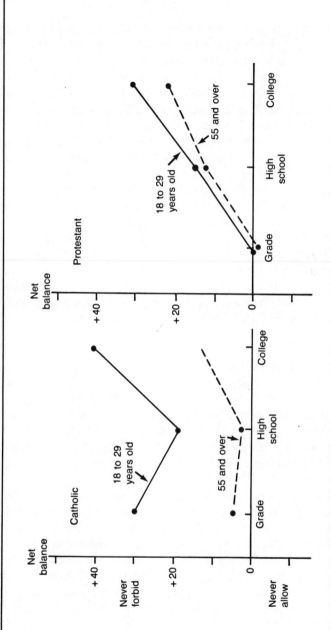

FIGURE 5–3 Attitudes toward Abortion among Young and Old Catholics and Protestants According to Education, 1984

ªPercentage "never forbid" minus "never allow" calculated over the total in each category.

Source: Center for Political Studies 1984 National Election Study.

pro-choice supporters in a group; a negative number indicates a pre-ponderance of pro-life supporters. As can be seen in Figure 5–3, for both the young and old, increasing education is accompanied by more support for the pro-choice position; furthermore, at each level of education the younger are more supportive than the older. The difference connected with age is rather slight among Protestants but quite dramatic among Catholics. In fact, young Catholics are more pro-choice on the abortion issue than young Protestants. These data do not take into account intensity of feelings and it is intensity that may, indeed, determine what ultimately transpires on this issue.

It is important to appreciate that there is no very strong relationship among a set of attitudes that might appear to be interconnected. Attitudes toward abortion, toward passage of the Equal Rights Amendment, and toward women's role in society are not highly related for the general public. Furthermore, no single attitude toward women appears to be strongly associated with other issue domains. Presumably this is an issue area where many nonpolitical influences are at work, and most people do not respond to such matters in a political way.

Foreign Affairs

Like noneconomic domestic problems, issues of foreign affairs vary greatly in salience, particularly in response to involvement of the nation in military conflicts. For brief periods, episodes like the hostage crisis in Iran are salient and extremely emotional but they may not have lasting effects. In recent years the most enduring issue of foreign policy was concern over military policies in Vietnam.[5]

As an issue of public policy, United States involvement in Vietnam has fascinating characteristics. Perhaps the most significant feature of public opinion over the Vietnam War is the sluggish pace with which awareness of the seriousness of American involvement developed and the slowness with which criticism and disenchantment with the course of the war in Vietnam increased. In 1964, more than one-third of the electorate had no opinion on questions about Vietnam, but by 1968, the proportion was reduced to only one in ten with no

---

[5]The most extensive analysis of attitudes toward the Vietnam War is found in John E. Mueller, *War, Presidents and Public Opinion* (New York: John Wiley & Sons, 1973). This work is all the more interesting because of a thorough comparison with public opinion during the Korean War.

opinion. The general public was much slower than opinion elites to respond to the issue.

One question the Survey Research Center consistently asked its national sample during this time was whether we did the right thing in getting involved in Vietnam or whether we should have stayed out. Over the course of the war, the percentage of the electorate responding that the United States should have stayed out of Vietnam rose from 24 percent in 1964 to 57 percent in 1972. To a slight degree Republicans were more likely to hold this view than Democrats prior to 1968, when the war was still "Johnson's war"; after the 1968 election, Democrats became somewhat more likely than Republicans to view the war as a mistake. This set of responses should not be interpreted as especially "dovish," since some people believed it had been a mistake to get involved, but once we were there, they believed we should win at all costs.

A better indication of hawk-dove sentiment is given by the responses to a second question, shown in Figure 5–4, asking whether the United States should pull out immediately or take a stronger stand,

FIGURE 5–4 Attitudes toward U.S. Involvement in Vietnam, 1964–1972

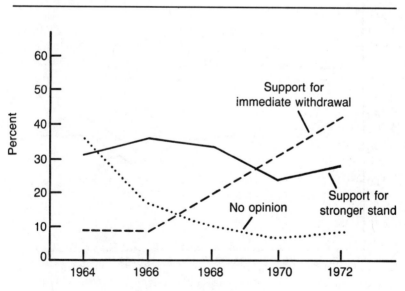

Source: Survey Research Center/Center for Political Studies National Election Studies.

even if it meant invading North Vietnam. Not shown in the figure are the large but declining proportions of respondents who favored the existing policy of the administration over either alternative. Support for a stronger stand remained stable after 1964, with about one-third of the electorate favoring an escalation of the war. In earlier years, popular support for prompt withdrawal was low, less than 10 percent; but by 1968, it had grown to 20 percent and increased more rapidly after that. By 1970, support for withdrawal was over 30 percent; by 1972, it was over 40 percent. In social science jargon, the issue became more polarized as it became more salient.

In 1968, Democrats and Republicans did not differ in their attitudes toward Vietnam, but independents tended to be more hawkish than either Democrats or Republicans. By 1972, the Democrats were substantially more dovish than the Republicans. Of all the issues examined in 1972 by the Center for Political Studies, Vietnam was most strongly associated with party identification. From this perspective, the election of Nixon in 1968 and his continuation of the war, even

FIGURE 5–5 Dovish Attitudes toward Vietnam According to Age, 1968 and 1972

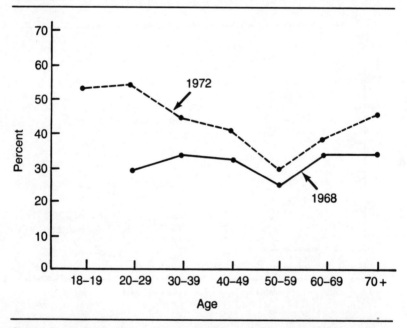

Source: Survey Research Center/Center for Political Studies National Election Studies.

while winding it down, permitted Democrats to shift further and faster to oppose continued American involvement. However, the Nixon administration's policy of deescalation permitted Republicans to shift in the same direction, but more cautiously.

Since so much attention has been given to young antiwar activists, it may be surprising to discover that only as the war was ending did doves begin to outnumber hawks among the young. College students are a minority of this age group, but according to surveys by the Gallup Poll, even college students were hawkish prior to 1968.[6] While the war was at its height, young Americans showed no tendency to be more dovish than any other age group, as can be seen in Figure 5–5. In fact, responses to other questions asked during that period showed the youngest members of the electorate to be the most hawkish and the elderly to be the most dovish. All this changed after 1968. Figure 5–5 shows that all groups moved in favor of immediate withdrawal, but young people made the trek in a dovish direction in much greater

FIGURE 5-6 Attitudes toward Foreign Aid and Increased Spending for Military, 1973–1983

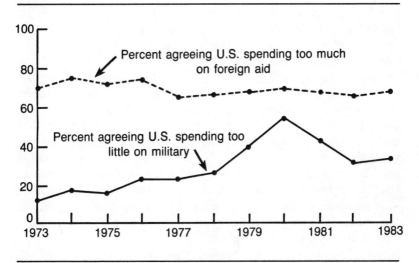

Source: General Social Surveys, 1972–1983 Cumulative Codebook, published by the National Opinion Research Center, University of Chicago, 1983.

[6]*The Gallup Opinion Index* (Princeton, N.J.: Gallup International, 1970), Report No. 55, January 1970, p. 16.

numbers. By the 1972 election, the youngest age groups were the most dovish of any age category.

The general aversion to the American experience in Vietnam was reflected in public attitudes toward defense spending as well. By the campaign of 1980, however, concern had grown over the seeming incapacity of the United States to react quickly and effectively in situations like the Iranian hostage crisis. As Figure 5-6 reveals, a temporary increase in the public's support for military spending occurred in 1979 and 1980. By 1982, as large increases in military spending were undertaken by the Reagan administration, support for further military spending declined to previous levels and more people favored reducing spending than increasing it. Regardless of this shift in opinion, the Reagan administration held to its original policy position.

Political Ideology

A political ideology is a set of fundamental beliefs or principles about the goals of political or governmental action and, often, about the proper procedures for the making of governmental decisions. Such an ideology provides the individual with a basic and reasonably long-term perspective for understanding and evaluating current issues and events. In this sense, ideology can serve a function for the individual similar to that of partisanship. In the case of ideology, however, the frame of reference consists of more abstract principles.

In the United States the most prominent current ideological patterns are those captured by the terms *liberalism* and *conservatism*. Although these words are used in a variety of ways, it would be commonly agreed that liberal ideology endorses the idea of social change and advocates the involvement of government in effecting such change, whereas conservatism seeks to defend the status quo and prescribes a more limited role for governmental activity. Another common conception of the terms portrays liberalism as advocating equality and individual freedom and conservatism endorsing a more ordered society; however, these dimensions are not always joined in the political thinking of Americans. Also, some evidence indicates that since the election campaign of 1964 the terms have become increasingly associated with attitudes on racial integration. To complicate the matter further, public opinion data suggest that a segment of the American electorate uses these terms to signify a set of social attitudes or life style rather than any particular political beliefs.

Despite these ambiguities, most commentators on the American political scene—not to mention the active participants—describe much of what happens in terms of liberalism or conservatism. Political history (and current news analysis) portrays situations in terms of a "trend toward conservatism," "middle-of-the-road policies," and "rejection of liberalism." Analysts characterize candidates and political parties as liberal or conservative. Within each party, leaders and platforms are alleged to be relatively liberal or conservative. The election and presidency of Ronald Reagan, for example, have been characterized as representing a "shift to the right" by the American public.

The major problems are to assess the importance of this variable for mass public opinion, to decide whether individuals in society are self-consciously oriented to politics as liberals, middle-of-the-roaders, or conservatives, and to determine whether individuals use this ideological orientation to organize political information and attitudes. In other words, does political ideology play a role for Americans similar to the role of partisanship as a basic determinant of their specific political views? In the remainder of this chapter, three kinds of evidence for the extent of ideological thinking in the American electorate will be considered: the use of ideological concepts in discussing politics; the consistency of attitudes on related issues suggesting an underlying perspective in the individual's approach to politics; and the individu-

TABLE 5-2 Levels of Conceptualization in the American Electorate, 1956 to 1980

Levels of Conceptual-ization	1956	1960	1964	1968	1972	1976	1980
Ideologues	12%	19%	27%	26%	22%	21%	21%
Group Benefits	42	31	27	24	27	26	31
Nature of Times	24	26	20	29	34	30	31
No Issue Content	22	23	26	21	17	24	17
Total	100%	99%	100%	100%	100%	101%	100%
n =	(1740)	(1741)	(1431)	(1319)	(1372)	(2870)	(1535)

Source: Angus Campbell et al., *The American Voter* (New York: John Wiley & Sons, 1960), p. 249, for 1956; Paul R. Hagner and John C. Pierce, "Conceptualization and Consistency in Political Beliefs: 1956–1976," paper presented at the Midwest Political Science Association meeting, 1981, p. 29, for 1960 to 1976; personal communication from John C. Pierce for 1980.

al's identification of himself or herself and the parties as liberal or conservative.

Survey Research Center data reported in *The American Voter* show that very few members of the electorate discuss their evaluations of the parties and the candidates in ideological language; only 12 percent did so in 1956.[7] The work of John Pierce and others has contributed to similar analysis of subsequent years.[8] As Table 5–2 shows, a change occurred in 1964. In fact, the proportions of "ideologues" doubled in 1964 over 1956 but still constituted only about one quarter of the electorate. This does not mean that most voters have no notions about what the parties stand for or what they are likely to do when in office. Large proportions of the electorate evaluate the parties with group symbols: "The Democrats help the working man" and "Republicans are good for business." Still there is a general lack of commitment to some set of abstract principles about the role of government in society on the basis of which the parties are evaluated.

Of course, individuals may be simply unsophisticated in the verbal descriptions of their feelings about politics and political parties. They may have an ideology that guides their political decisions but they are unable to articulate it. In that case, the individual's attitudes toward public issues might be expected to show a degree of coherence and consistency, since those positions would be arrived at through the application of a common underlying set of political ideals. If individuals are liberal on one issue, one would expect them to be liberal on other related issues; if they are conservative on one, they would be conservative on others. The most sophisticated analysis of ideological perspectives and consistency in issue positions, usually called *issue constraint*, was carried out by Philip Converse on Survey Research Center data from 1956, 1958, and 1960.[9] He found that the strength of relationship among domestic issues and among foreign policy issues was about twice as strong as the relationship between domestic and

[7]Angus Campbell et al., *The American Voter* (New York: John Wiley & Sons, 1960), p. 249.

[8]John C. Pierce, "Ideology, Attitudes and Voting Behavior of the American Electorate: 1956, 1960, 1964" (Ph.D. diss., University of Minnesota, 1969), Table 3.1,, p. 63; Paul R. Hagner and John C. Pierce, "Conceptualization and Consistency in Political Beliefs: 1956–1976," paper presented at the Midwest Political Science Association meeting, 1981. See also Norman H. Nie, Sidney Verba, and John R. Petrocik, *The Changing American Voter* (Cambridge, Mass.: Harvard University Press, 1976), chap. 7.

[9]Philip E. Converse, "The Nature of Belief Systems in Mass Publics," in Apter (ed.), *Ideology and Discontent*, pp. 238–245.

foreign issues. By normal standards even the strongest relationship among domestic issues did not suggest particularly impressive issue consistency.

More recently Nie and Andersen augmented this analysis with the addition of another decade of coverage.[10] As with several other patterns, a change occurred during the campaign of 1964. The degree of issue constraint on various policy matters increased in 1964 and remains higher than in the earlier era. This change has been variously interpreted as (1) a result of the increased distinctiveness of the parties, (2) the increasing salience of race, or (3) measurement error.[11]

In a recent analysis of data collected by the Center for Political Studies for a panel survey in 1972, 1974, and 1976, Converse and Markus found that the instability of attitudes on policy issues was remarkably similar to the pattern of the late 1950s.[12] They concluded that there was no evidence of basic change in issue constraint in the 1970s. Americans have less stable attitudes on policy matters than, say, on party identification and the issues that are likely to be of low concern to most people, such as foreign aid, reveal the most volatility. Views on a salient, emotional matter like school busing remained much more consistent over the four-year period.

As might be expected, the degree of consistency among attitudes on different issues varies with the level of education of the individual, the more educated being substantially more consistent in their views than the less educated. However, increasing levels of education do not appear to account for the increase in issue constraint over the last decade. The work of Nie and Andersen shows convincingly that interest in politics is more critical.[13] In other words, as the public becomes more concerned with issues and more attentive to political leaders,

[10]Norman H. Nie and Kristi Andersen, "Mass Belief Systems Revisited: Political Change and Attitude Structure," *Journal of Politics* 36 (September 1974): 541–591.

[11]John L. Sullivan, James E. Piereson, and George E. Marcus, "Ideological Constraint in the Mass Public: A Methodological Critique and Some New Findings," *American Journal of Political Science* 22 (May 1978): 233–249; George F. Bishop, Alfred J. Tuchfarber, and Robert W. Oldendick, "Change in the Structure of American Political Attitudes: The Nagging Question of Question Wording," *American Journal of Political Science* 22 (May 1978): 250–269.

[12]Philip E. Converse and Gregory B. Markus, "Plus ça change...: The New CPS Election Study Panel," *The American Political Science Review* 73 (March 1979): 32–49.

[13]Nie and Andersen, "Mass Beliefs Systems Revisited: Political Change and Attitude Structure."

the public perceives a higher degree of issue coherence. Almost certainly the electorate generally has the capacity for greater issue constraint than shown in recent decades; however, the exercise of this capacity depends much more on political leaders and events than on the characteristics of the electorate. When political leaders use ideological terms to describe themselves and the clusters of issues that they support, the electorate is quite capable of following suit.

The degree of issue constraint will, of course, depend on the range of issues considered. Even in the 1950s, *The American Voter* documents a rather coherent set of attitudes on welfare policies and governmental activity. When the analysis moves to more disparate issues, such as support for welfare policies and support for civil liberties, the relationships weaken substantially. It can be argued, of course, that little relationship should be expected between positions in these different issue areas because they tap different ideological dimensions with no logical or necessary connection among them. Thus there is nothing logically inconsistent in a person's opposing government regulation of business and believing in racial equality. Conversely, as the enforcement of antidiscrimination laws more and more involves trade unions and schools, the pattern of the economic liberal who opposes civil rights becomes more familiar. In foreign policy, the Vietnam War did much to rearrange old notions of what is "liberal" and what is "conservative." On other issues of foreign policy, such as military and economic foreign aid, international trade, and relations with Russia and China, internationalist views have generally been considered the liberal position and isolationist attitudes conservative. Even among political leaders, the connection between positions on foreign policy and views on domestic economic policy has never been universal, but it has not even been a weak relationship in the general public. In considering the question of issue constraint, two points thus should be kept in mind: (1) the meaning of the terms *liberal* and *conservative* change with time, as do the connections between these ideologies and specific historical events; and (2) analysts, in studying issue constraint, invariably impose on the analysis their own version of ideological consistency, which, in light of the ambiguities surrounding the terms, is likely to be somewhat artificial.

In general, American attitudes on public issues do not fit into a neat ordering on a liberal-conservative ideological continuum. Or, to put it differently, Americans are neither consistently liberal nor conservative on a wide range of issues. One individual may be liberal on economic issues, conservative on race relations, moderate on foreign policy, and so on. Another individual might be liberal on civil rights, moderate on welfare matters, and conservative on foreign policy. When viewed collectively, the opinions of these individuals form no single, consistent pattern, even though each individual's attitudes might be reasonable enough for him or her.

Ideological Identification

A somewhat less strenuous requirement for ideological orientation is to ask individuals whether they ever think of themselves as liberal or conservative. When Americans are asked to identify themselves in this way, most are able to do so. The categories obviously have some meaning for many Americans; the identifications simply are not of overriding importance. In recent years many Americans have tended to think of themselves as conservative. Commercial public opinion polls have regularly shown that larger proportions call themselves conservatives than liberals. During the past decade or so there has been little change in the ideological identification of the electorate. Basically, the pattern is one of stability; there is no evidence of a shift to the right.

It is also possible to draw on the 1984 study by the Center for Political Studies to investigate the relationship between ideological self-identification and partisan self-identification. Table 5–3 shows that Democrats are more liberal than conservative, Republicans are disproportionately conservative, and independents are slightly conservative. But conservatives are twice as likely to be Republican as Democratic, and liberals are much more likely to be Democrats.

TABLE 5–3 The Relationship between Ideological Self-Identification and Party Identification, 1984

	Democrats	Independents	Republicans	
Liberal	14%	8	4	26%
Middle-of-the-road	13	12	7	32%
Conservative	9	13	21	43%
	36%	33%	32%	
n = 1395*				

*Omits "no opinion" and "don't know."

Source: Center for Political Studies 1984 National Election Study.

The relationship between ideology and partisanship is shown in the low coincidence of Republican and liberal identifications.

Also, the electorate tends to perceive the Democratic party as liberal and the Republican party as conservative. Understandably, this has the potential for creating some tension among conservative Democrats and liberal Republicans. Of course, these partisans may perceive their party differently from most people; but in fact substantial numbers of partisans, Democrats mostly, appear to see themselves as much closer to the other party ideologically. Perhaps over the years this conflict undermines party loyalty, but in the short run it does not seem to have much impact.

If the way individuals perceive the parties ideologically is taken into account, the relationship between partisanship and ideological self-identification becomes somewhat more consistent. This is the result of southern conservative Democrats seeing the Democratic party as more conservative than the Republican party. In many areas of the South, this probably is an accurate perception.

There is no similar relationship between social class and ideological self-identification; in fact, there is no relationship at all. By way of contrast, educational and ethnic groups differ considerably in their ideological outlook. Figure 5–7 reveals that self-identified liberals are most frequent among blacks and Jews, whereas self-identified conservatives are common among college-educated whites in both North and South. There is some tendency for Catholics at all levels of education to be more liberal than Protestants. The middle-of-the-road position tends to be taken by the less well educated.

Since American political parties, and American politics in general, have usually been regarded as extremely nonideological, strong relationships between class, party, and ideology should not be expected. Ideology and issue positions are another matter. There is a consistent relationship in the expected direction between self-proclaimed ideology and positions on issues. Table 5–4 shows the relationship between ideological identification and liberal views on policy matters in various years and a dovish position on Vietnam in 1972. Even though we must keep in mind that about one-third of the sample do not have an ideological position or do not profess attitudes on these issues and are missing in this analysis, Table 5–4 documents strong, consistent relationships between ideological identification and many issue positions. The data do not, however, demonstrate that ideology determines issue positions.

If everyone had a strong ideology, attitudes would be determined by that ideology. To a considerable extent, this appears to happen to

FIGURE 5–7 Ideological Self-Identification According to Region, Race, Religion, and Education, 1984

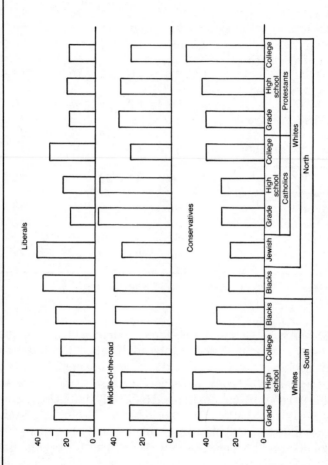

Source: Center for Political Studies 1984 National Election Study.

TABLE 5-4 The Relationship between Ideological Self-Identification and Liberal Positions on Issues of Public Policy, 1972–1984

	Very Liberal	Middle-of-the-road			Very Conservative
Defense Spending (1984)	62	43	32	24	19
Maintaining Services (1984)	71	68	53	44	35
Abortion (1984)	60	50	39	35	28
Government guarantee of jobs (1984)	52	36	28	20	19
Getting along with Russia (1984)	65	52	34	33	20
Equal Rights Amendment (1980)	91	78	64	48	38
Prayer in schools (1980)	57	41	24	30	14
Protect rights of accused (1976)	59	41	29	22	20
Government medical insurance (1976)	66	45	33	27	16
Legalize marijuana (1976)	60	49	24	24	10
Tax rates (1972)	52	41	36	30	29
Vietnam (1972)	75	61	39	33	27

Source: Center for Political Studies National Election Studies.

the most politically alert and concerned in our society, but this group is only a very small minority of the total adult population. If the major American political parties were ideologically oriented, then by following the parties or political leaders in these parties, Americans would have their opinions determined indirectly by ideology. But the two major political parties are notoriously nonideological. Many of the leaders have personal ideological commitments, but no single ideology dominates either party. Usually specific matters of public policy are of little interest to the electorate; as a consequence, the political parties are unconcerned with dramatizing particular policies.

Quite a bit has been written about this interrelationship between party, ideology, and issue positions, and much remains in dispute. It is safe to say that any one of the three factors can influence the other two, and in extreme cases one factor could completely determine the other two. Surely some extreme partisans alter their ideology and issue stands to conform to their party; and some ideologues switch or abandon parties and take issue positions in strict conformity with the dictates of their ideology. Finally, some people doubtless feel so strongly about one or more issues that they will change both party and ideology to correspond to an issue position. Everything known about the American public, however, suggests that few care so intensely about either party or ideology or issues. Typically, one factor has little causal impact on another. Most people rarely find themselves in such a position that feelings are so strong and views so clearly focused that they must greatly adjust their attitudes and identifications. But in those rare cases when individuals feel that important interests are at stake, it is most unlikely that party loyalty or ideological beliefs will overcome strongly felt interests.

6

Vote Choice and Electoral Decisions

———————— ☆☆☆ ————————

The central focus of research on American political behavior is vote choice, especially presidential vote choice. No other single form of mass political activity has the popular interest or analytic significance that surrounds the selection of a president every four years. Most Americans follow presidential campaigns with greater attention than they give other elections, and eventually over 50 percent of the electorate expresses a preference by voting. The results of presidential balloting are reported and analyzed far more extensively than any others. This chapter will explore the main determinants of vote choice and the interpretation of electoral decisions in light of these determinants. An attempt will be made to generalize the discussion beyond presidential vote choice, but inevitably most of the illustrations are drawn from recent presidential election studies.

Earlier chapters have emphasized party loyalty as a basic characteristic that influences many aspects of an individual's political behavior. In regard to vote choice, an individual's partisanship can be construed as a long-term predisposition to vote for one party or another, other things being equal. In other words, in the absence of any information about candidates and issues or other "short-term forces" in an election, individuals can be expected to vote according to their partisanship. On the other hand, to the extent that such short-term forces have an impact on them, they may be deflected away from their usual

121

party loyalty toward some other action. Clearly, more potent short-term forces would be required to cause a very strong partisan to vote for another party than would be necessary to lead a weak partisan to defect. An individual's vote in an election can be viewed as the product of the strength of his partisanship and the impact of the short-term forces on the individual.

In most elections, both candidates and political commentators give their attention to short-term forces, such as the personalities of the candidates, issues, and the parties' records, since these are the variable elements that the actions of candidates and campaign strategies seek to modify. Although in many respects partisanship is the most important element, it is taken as a constant since, in the short run, it is not likely to change. This chapter will consider the impact of the short-term forces of candidate image, current party images, and issues within a setting of stable party loyalties.

Candidate Image

The appeal of candidates has been given more attention than any other short-term influences in recent elections. It is practically impossible to isolate the differential reactions to personalities of candidates prior to the era of survey research, but during the past twenty years national samples have been extensively questioned about likes and dislikes concerning the presidential candidates. This period also has provided several very popular candidates with extremely favorable images, as well as several who were rejected by the electorate largely on the basis of their personal attributes.

The specific content of candidates' images has varied greatly, and, as Figure 6-1 shows, no single pattern appears associated with either party. In 1952 and 1956, Dwight Eisenhower was widely perceived to be an excellent as well as extremely likable candidate. On many personality characteristics he was perceived much more favorably than his opponent, Adlai Stevenson. A large proportion of the favorable and unfavorable references to Eisenhower in 1952 had to do with his experience as a military man; but by 1956, he was perceived almost entirely in other terms, mainly that of personal charm rather than experience or qualifications.

In several elections Richard Nixon enjoyed a more favorable image than his various opponents. Although most American voters would soon revise their evaluations, in 1960 Nixon was more favorably perceived in personal terms than John Kennedy; his personal

FIGURE 6-1 Images of the Democratic and Republican Presidential Candidates, 1952–1984

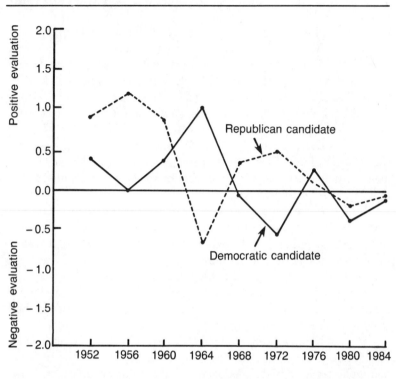

Source: Warren E. Miller, Arthur H. Miller, and Edward J. Schneider, *American National Election Studies Data Sourcebook* (Cambridge, Mass.: Harvard University Press, 1980), pp. 127, 129; Center for Politcal Studies National Election Studies.

image rivaled Eisenhower's. Kennedy's image improved during his presidency, but his extraordinary popularity came after his assassination.

Sometimes a candidate enjoys an advantage over an opponent because the opponent is extremely unpopular; in recent years Lyndon Johnson had such an advantage over Barry Goldwater, as did Richard Nixon over George McGovern. In 1964, the only strong point in Goldwater's image was "integrity," whereas many unfavorable references were made to personal characteristics like "impulsiveness" and being "trigger-happy." In 1972, McGovern was held in very low esteem; only about one-third of the public thought he could be trusted as president. Almost 60 percent thought Nixon could be trusted; and George Wallace, although no longer a candidate, was viewed as more trustworthy than McGovern.

In 1976, both Ford and Carter were, on balance, perceived positively—the first time that had happened to both major candidates since 1960. The response to Ford personally, however, was barely more positive than negative and Carter's image was not much more favorable. The most common negative references were to Carter's lack of credibility although, on the whole, more voters saw him as honest than dishonest. Carter also was positively evaluated as being religious, a characteristic that usually has not figured in the evaluation of candidates. Ford's overall image was remarkably lacking in issue content apart from negative reaction to his having granted a pardon to former President Nixon.

By 1980, the electorate's view of Carter had changed. On balance, his image became more negative than positive and a large proportion of the public considered him weak and indecisive. Like other incumbent presidents before him, in the 1980 election Carter was viewed favorably in terms of having had experience, and he was seen by many people as having integrity. John Anderson also had a slightly more unfavorable than favorable image, although many people had trouble thinking of anything to say about him.

In both 1980 and 1984, the public's view of Reagan was more negative than positive. In both years a very large share of the negative comments referred to Reagan's age and while many people mentioned this point, it does not seem to have been an intensely unfavorable evaluation. Many of the positive views of Reagan in 1984 were equally mild expressions of approval of the way he was handling his job as president. One might say that Reagan did not need to be seen favorably because he had the good fortune to face opponents who were even more negatively evaluated by the public. Mondale, like Carter, was viewed as weak; in addition, many people thought Mondale was dishonest or unprincipled. In the elections of 1980 and 1984, all the candidates were viewed more negatively than positively, which represents a new low in candidate appeal for recent decades.

This analysis, which simply counts the numbers of positive and negative comments, should be viewed cautiously since the relative seriousness of the complaints—for example, being old versus being unprincipled—is not taken into account. Still, the fact that people found more negative than positive things to say about Reagan casts a somewhat different light on the "enormous personal popularity" he is generally thought to have.

Very few candidates for other offices are as well known or as well publicized as candidates for the presidency. Most candidates in most elections are unknown quantities for the average voter. Typically, voters will be aware of the candidate's party affiliation and whether or not he or she is an incumbent, but not much more. And these elements of information may come to the attention of the voter only if they are indicated on the ballot.

Normally, the impact of candidate image on vote choice declines as one goes further down the ticket to less visible and less well-known offices. This does not mean that the candidate's personal qualities are unimportant in winning election to these offices. They may be of paramount importance in obtaining the nomination or endorsement of the party organization, in raising financial support, in putting together a campaign staff, and in gaining backing from the leadership of influential organizations. But these personal attributes are unlikely to influence the decisions of the average voter simply because the voter is unlikely to be aware of them.

Selling Presidential Candidates

A good bit of nonsense has been written in recent years about winning elections by manipulating the images of the candidates, mainly through the mass media. The implication has been that the images of candidates are easily created and altered, but actually to do either one appears difficult and expensive. Some elements in candidate images may be susceptible to manipulation through skillful public relations work, but many elements are not.[1] In 1960, Kennedy's Catholicism prompted both positive and negative reactions, but these impressions could not have been controlled or altered much by the candidates or their agents. The Kennedy organization did have some choices about making an issue of religion; but once the decisions were made, there was less leeway in controlling the impact of the issue. In most other cases, the candidates have little control in deciding whether to raise certain topics, for often the opponent will do so anyway. In 1972, McGovern could do little about the impression he created by dropping Eagleton from the ticket, nor could Ford erase the effects of his

---

[1]Some good research on the media and politics is available. See, for example, Kurt Lang and Gladys Engel Lang, *Politics and Television* (Chicago: Quadrangle Books, 1968). For a scholarly survey of campaign techniques, see Dan Nimmo, *The Political Persuaders* (Englewood Cliffs, N.J.: Prentice-Hall, 1970).

pardoning of Nixon. Carter could not create the impression that the hostages were free while they were still held in Teheran.

The Carter administration as much as any up to that point had faith in the power of media image-building, announcing at one point that henceforth it would project an image of greater decisiveness to the American public. But as Carter discovered, image is rarely a substitute for the genuine article. The public's impressions of candidates for major office seem to be realistic, gained primarily through ordinary news coverage. This is not to say that these images are completely accurate or fair or sophisticated, but neither are they fictitious pictures created by public relations personnel. An incumbent candidate or a former vice-president benefits from a perception of being experienced, which is not purely a result of campaign advertising. On the other hand, he cannot entirely escape any negative reactions that might be aroused by his involvement in an unpopular administration, as Carter found in 1980 and as Humphrey found in 1968.

A necessary condition for the successful selling of a candidate with advertising techniques requires that the image makers be able to control the information available about their candidate, thereby controlling the perceptions of the voters about him. For a relatively unknown challenger, like McGovern or Carter in 1976, such a strategy would appear self-defeating, since no candidate has the resources to become well-known nationwide through advertising and staged appearances alone. Instead, unknowns must scramble for exposure in any forum they can find, and this prevents the careful manipulation of an image. On the other hand, well-known candidates or incumbents who can afford to sit back and let the public relations people campaign for them by virtue of being known to the electorate, already have images that are probably impossible to modify in significant ways over the relatively short time available in an election campaign. The most famous alleged attempt to "sell" a candidate was the effort of the Nixon campaign staff in the 1968 presidential election. However, the evidence suggests that more voters decided to vote for other candidates during the course of the campaign than decided to vote for Richard Nixon. After almost twenty years of nationwide public exposure, a "new Nixon" reinforced existing images, both negative and positive; he could not create a new, more favorable image.

In the rare case in which a virtual unknown gains rapid political prominence without the usual exposure, the lack of information about him or her allows public attitudes to fluctuate. In 1974, when Gerald Ford became president, he was not well known to the American public. The highly favorable but rather vague impression of him that accompanied his taking office changed dramatically within a month when he pardoned Nixon. Early in 1976, Jimmy Carter was little known and public perceptions of him varied widely. After his nomination, however, he was much more clearly perceived by the public, although uncertainty over his issue positions was confessed to by his supporters as well as his detractors. The relatively small amount of information available to the public about Carter prior to the start of the campaign made his early support subject to erosion. Since attitudes about him were not well formed, the information gained through the course of the campaign had a potentially greater impact on his popularity than it would have had on a better-known candidate.

The perceptions voters had of Gary Hart during the primaries in 1984 were reminiscent of those of Carter in 1976. Hart's image changed dramatically in a short time as he moved from an unknown to a front-runner to an also-ran. Hart was known to very few Americans in early February. By the end of the month, due to the media attention he received after the Iowa caucuses, he was widely known and viewed more positively by Democrats and independents than his major opponent, Walter Mondale. In another month, his recognition among the public had increased further, but his popularity sagged and he again trailed Mondale among Democrats. Once people were aware of him, Hart's popularity appeared to vary, as much as anything, with the perceived likelihood of his getting the Democratic nomination.

Attitudes toward Geraldine Ferraro displayed a similar volatility. When, as a virtual unknown, she was picked by Mondale as his running mate, the response was overwhelmingly favorable; as questions began to be raised about her husband's business dealings, her approval ratings quickly turned downward and she went from being seen as an asset to the ticket to a liability. In contrast to both Hart and Ferraro, Mondale, as a former vice-president, was very well known long before the primary campaign began in 1984. Continuous monitoring of Mondale's image through surveys conducted from January to November by the Center for Political Studies reveals a very high degree of stability.

In a study of presidential campaigns through 1976, Benjamin Page showed that the attempts by candidates to change their images resulted in a perceived loss of integrity.[2] In particular, candidates who

---

[2]Benjamin I. Page, *Choices and Echoes in Presidential Elections* (Chicago: University of Chicago Press, 1978).

thought they needed to move toward the middle of the political spectrum were perceived as waffling on the issues.

Ronald Reagan was more successfully handled as a candidate than most of his predecessors. Perhaps his professional training as an actor made him more susceptible to management by his advisors. But, to a considerable degree, image-building for a political figure like Reagan depends on protecting him from the press and public exposure rather than manipulating publicity by "selling" particular content. This approach was especially effective in the campaign of 1980 when the focus of attention and dissatisfaction was on President Carter. As president, Reagan has been quite inaccessible and there have been few uncontrolled public appearances. President Reagan did not campaign as extensively in 1984 as he had in 1980 and, with a large lead in the polls, there was little pressure to do so.

There are other circumstances in which public relations and mass-advertising techniques could conceivably be successful in foisting a candidate on an unwitting public. In a single state a previously unknown candidate could saturate the mass media with prepackaged information. If the opponent were likewise unknown and without the financial resources to wage a countercampaign, such a strategy might well succeed. This is particularly true in party primaries or in nonpartisan elections in which the partisanship of the candidate does not become involved in the evaluation of his attributes. A variant of this strategy became commonplace in the 1980 campaign in several Senate races. Conservative Political Action Committees (PACs) spent large amounts of money to create *negative* images of the liberal incumbents. Not only were the mass media used extensively and skillfully, but the PACs also had the "advantage" of operating independently of the little-known challengers in these races. Seeds of doubt thus could be planted about the incumbent's personal characteristics and record without having to accomplish the more difficult task of building a positive image for the challenger. The issue of the media and its impact on political attitudes will be returned to in Chapter 7.

Party Images

The images of the parties are another factor that can influence the voting decisions of the electorate. Even though party images are strongly colored by long-standing party loyalties, the focus of this analysis is a set of potentially variable attitudes toward the parties that can be viewed as short-run forces at work in an election. Party images also affect and are affected by the images of the candidates running under the party label and by the attitudes toward issues espoused by the candidates or the party platforms. These factors can be kept distinct conceptually, though it may be impossible to disentangle the various effects in any actual situation. In the perceptions of the electorate, the parties are distinct in ideology and on most issues.

Figure 6–2 shows the changing perceptions of the parties' abilities to keep the country out of war. Traditionally, the Republican party has been favored in this area during presidential contests, with the advantage being reversed twice in the past twenty years, once in 1964 by the candidacy of Goldwater and again during the Carter and first Reagan administrations. In 1985, the Republican party once again was viewed as the party better able to keep the country out of war.

Until recently the Democratic party has been viewed fairly consistently as the party of prosperity. There are brief lapses in this pattern, displayed in Figure 6–3, but overall the Democrats have enjoyed a clear advantage over the Republicans. With the beginning of the Reagan administration, the Republicans became the party of prosperity in the public's view. This image lasted through 1981 and then reverted for two years as the economy slid into recession. In 1984 and 1985, the Republican party's image as the party of prosperity was restored by margins greater than either party had enjoyed since before 1980.

Twice since World War II a party has acquired an unfavorable image as corrupt and dishonest. To a moderate degree the Truman administration was so perceived in the late forties and early fifties. This perception was in addition to the common impression that any administration is guilty of some corruption. But the negative perceptions of this sort in early years were nothing compared with the party image of the Republicans after the Watergate scandals. At least for a while the Republican party had to operate with an extraordinary handicap in image.

Party images are strongly related to partisanship, with partisans more likely to embrace positive images of their party and to reject negative ones than independents or partisans of the opposition. On the other hand, partisanship and party image are not synonymous, for individuals often share unfavorable perceptions of their party without changing party identification. At some point, however, negative images of one's own party or positive perceptions of the other party undoubtedly lead to partisan change.

The images of local or state parties may be considerably different from and independent of those of their national counterpart. The

130

FIGURE 6–2 Attitudes on Which Party Is More Likely to Keep the Country Out of War, 1939–1985

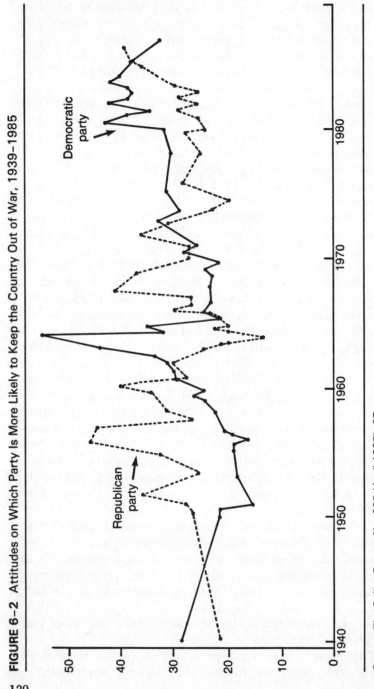

Source: The Gallup Report, No. 235 (April 1985): 27.

FIGURE 6-3 Attitudes on Which Party Will Do a Better Job of Keeping the Country Prosperous, 1951-1985

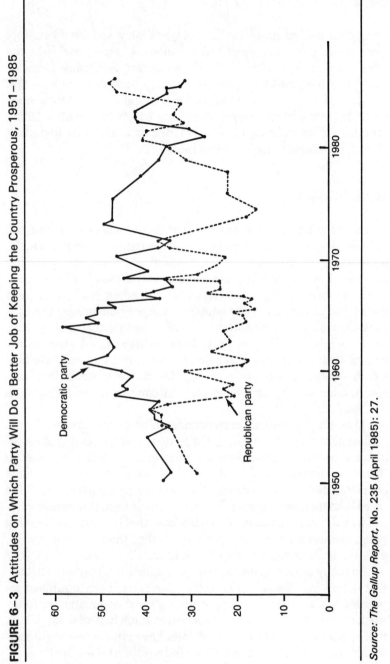

Source: *The Gallup Report*, No. 235 (April 1985): 27.

Chicago organization of the late Mayor Daley and the Mississippi Democratic party are perceived in different terms, one from the other, as well as from the national Democrats, and many a local or state party has gained a reputation for ineptitude or corruption that did not influence voting decisions for national offices. At the same time, these local images may become increasingly important in voting for offices at lower levels since party labels become a more important identifying characteristic in those races.

Issue Impact

Obviously, candidate images and party images may be closely related to issues, and under some circumstances are indistinguishable. On the other hand, the perception of the stands of candidates and parties on issues is a basis for making vote choices, a basis usually distinct from either personality characteristics or long-standing symbolism. Most significantly, candidates can establish issue positions or alter their appeals through their presentation of issues in ways that are not applicable to personal images or party characteristics. Candidates cannot change their experience or religion or party, but they can take new stands on issues or attempt to change the salience of issues. It is feasible, in other words, for candidates to attempt to appeal for votes on the basis of issues.

Over the past several years, considerable commentary has focused on the rise of single-issue voting. Collections of voters, caring intensely about a particular issue, vote for whichever candidate is closest to their views on that issue, regardless of the candidate's party, personal characteristics, or positions on other issues. Actually there is nothing new about this phenomenon. The classic single issue of American politics was abolition, an issue of such intensity that it destroyed the Whig party, launched several new parties including the Republican party, and was a major contributing factor to the Civil War.

In many areas and for many voters, abortion is currently an issue that determines the vote they will cast. Although organizational sophistication and increased opportunities for dissemination of information make single-issue groups a potent force in American politics today, politically ambitious candidates have always searched for issues of this type to help them gain a following. At the same time, incumbent candidates and the broadly based political parties have seen advantages in avoiding or glossing over such issues. Intense concentration on a single issue is potentially divisive and damaging to parties that must appeal to a broad range of voters or to those in office who must cast votes on a wide range of issues. Nevertheless, the political opportunity for the candidate who can capture a group of voters willing to vote on the basis of a single issue or cluster of issues is so great that it is unlikely that any intense concern in the electorate will be long ignored.

Several characteristics of electoral behavior conflict with this description of the role of issues in influencing vote choice. For one thing, in most elections many voters are unaware of the stands taken by candidates on issues. Finding that voters believe the candidates they support agree with them on issues is common. This suggests that voters may project their issue positions onto their favorite candidate more often than they decide to vote for candidates on the basis of their position on issues. Furthermore, when voters agree on issues with the candidate they support, they may have adopted this position merely in order to agree with their candidate. Actually, candidates and other political leaders frequently perform this function for members of the electorate; they provide issue leadership for their following.

During a campaign, individual voters can ordinarily be aroused to take a stand on some issues in support of their party or candidate and be made to care moderately about the issue. The voters recognize its importance but do not feel a great personal stake in the matter. A classic example of a campaign-inspired issue was the question raised in 1960 of whether to defend Quemoy and Matsu, two tiny islands between Taiwan and the People's Republic of China. The debate between the candidates on the topic caused well-informed and interested voters to take stands on the issue, but it is unlikely that many, including the candidates, ever felt intensely about it.

Among the enormous range of possible issues at any given time, complete indifference to many is quite common. Most issues important to political leaders remain in this category for the general public. Since World War II, American political leaders have found the public's lack of interest in foreign affairs quite frustrating. In general, American voters are assumed to care about domestic economic issues, if they care about any issue, and to be indifferent to foreign policy issues. A related but different emphasis casts this relationship in a broader pattern: voters care intensely about an issue when they are suffering or perceive a threat. Usually the easiest threat to understand is economic, whereas the most difficult threats to comprehend are in the area of foreign policy. Perhaps Vietnam as an issue had an easily understood, immediate meaning for those threatened by the draft or those close to someone serving in Vietnam. For most of the public,

Vietnam became meaningful because it lasted so long as an issue and probably because some elements of information about the war, like casualties, were made known so dramatically. Significantly, when the ground troops were removed from Vietnam, public concern over the war declined abruptly; once the issue no longer touched close to home, intensity of feeling over the continuing air war was confined to a relatively small segment of the public.

The extent to which voters are concerned with issues in making vote choices is a subject of considerable debate. Several recent scholarly efforts were designed to rescue the voter from an undeserved reputation for not being issue oriented.[3] *The Changing American Voter*[4] by Nie, Verba, and Petrocik documents a rise in issue voting associated with the election of 1964. According to their data, the correlation between attitudes on issues and vote choice peaked in the ideological Johnson-Goldwater campaign, but remained through 1972 at a considerably higher level than in the "issueless" 1950s. More recently, in a thorough assessment of the impact of issues in the Reagan elections of 1980 and 1984, Merrill Shanks and Warren Miller found relatively low levels of issue impact.[5]

A number of factors must be present for issues to have an impact on vote choice: first, the voters must be informed and concerned about an issue; second, the candidates must take distinguishable stands on this issue; and third, the voters must perceive the candidates' stands in relation to their own. The 1972 presidential election provided an example of a clear choice between candidates on an issue when McGovern was perceived as taking a dramatically different position on Vietnam than Nixon did. Figure 6–4 illustrates the electorate's perceptions of the stands of Nixon and McGovern on the Vietnam issue as well as the relationship between the voters' own stands on Vietnam and their choice between the two presidential candidates. In the 1972 survey, voters were asked to locate each candidate on a seven-point scale ranging from a position favoring "total withdraw-

---

[3]A good discussion of this topic in a single source is the collection of articles and commentary by Gerald Pomper, Richard Boyd, Richard Brody, Benjamin Page, and John Kessel in *American Political Science Review 66* (June 1972): 415–470. See also Page, *Choices and Echoes in Presidential Elections.*

[4]Norman H. Nie, Sidney Verba, and John R. Petrocik, *The Changing American Voter* (Cambridge, Mass.: Harvard University Press, 1976), chap. 10.

[5]J. Merrill Shanks and Warren E. Miller, "Policy Direction and Performance Evaluation: Complementary Explanations of the Reagan Elections," paper presented at the American Political Science Association meeting, 1985.

FIGURE 6–4 Vote for President According to Attitudes on Vietnam and Perceptions of Candidates' Position on That Issue, 1972

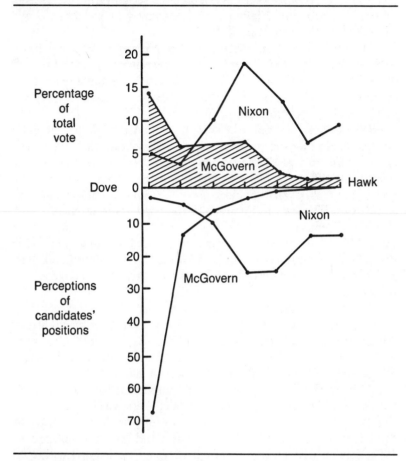

Source: Center for Political Studies 1972 National Election Study.

al from Vietnam" to "taking a stronger stand." In Figure 6–4, the frequency distributions in the lower half of the chart illustrate the voters' perceptions of the two candidates' locations on this Vietnam scale. The figure indicates, for example, that almost 70 percent of the public understood McGovern's position to be one of total withdrawal, with almost no one thinking that he favored taking a stronger stand. Perceptions of Nixon's position were more varied, but most placed him toward the "hawkish" end of the scale. Voters also were asked about their own position on Vietnam using the same seven-point scale. The frequency distributions in the upper half of the figure indicate the self-placements on the scale of Nixon and McGovern voters. It shows that McGovern drew most of his support from voters who shared his position on Vietnam, while Nixon's support came mainly from those in the middle positions.

The Vietnam issue in 1972 is a good example of the kind of pattern that would be expected if an issue is strongly related to voting for candidates: the voters perceive a clear distinction in the stands of the candidates on the issue, and voters' choices between candidates are related to their own positions on the issue.

The situation was quite different in 1968. Although the presidential election in that year was accompanied by an extremely high level of voter concern over Vietnam, many voters were unable to perceive a significant difference between Nixon and Humphrey on Vietnam policy. Thus, they were unable to base their choice on this salient concern.[6] As can be seen in Figure 6–5, the perceptions of Nixon's and Humphrey's stands on Vietnam were remarkably similar, and understandably the distribution of their vote reveals little association with the voters' positions on Vietnam. Wallace, on the other hand, was seen as offering a distinctively different position and, to a degree, this is reflected in the vote that he received.

There is some disagreement among analysts over the impact of issues on presidential vote choice in 1980; however, Shanks and Miller show that issues had even less effect in 1984.[7] Reagan's rating as president and voters' positive assessment of the condition of the country can be viewed as largely displacing issues in 1984.

Although many other factors had more influence than issues on the choice between Reagan and Mondale, there was still a relationship between some issues and vote choice for president. Contrary to the impression created by the candidates and the commentators in 1984, foreign policy issues were more strongly associated with vote choice than domestic economic issues like cutting government services. According to Shanks and Miller, attitudes toward defense spending had the greatest impact on vote choice in 1984. Those strongly favoring decreased military spending voted more than three to one for Mondale; those strongly favoring increased defense spend-

---

[6]Benjamin Page and Richard Brody, "Policy Voting and the Electoral Process: The Vietnam War Issue," *American Political Science Review* 66 (September 1972): 979–995.

[7]Shanks and Miller, "Policy Direction and Performance Evaluation: Complementary Explanations of the Reagan Elections."

FIGURE 6–5 Vote for President According to Attitudes on Vietnam and Perceptions of Candidates' Position on That Issue, 1968

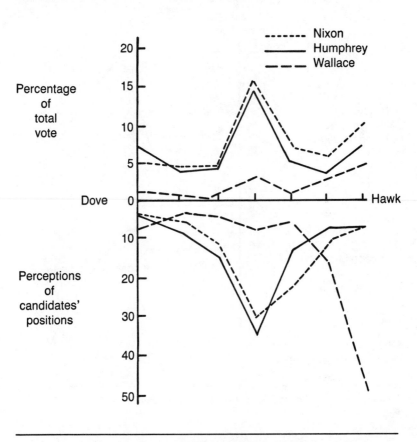

Source: Survey Research Center 1968 National Election Study.

ing voted just as onesidedly for Reagan. The relationship weakens among those with more moderate opinions.

Very few of the voters who supported President Reagan were in favor of cutting defense spending, as indicated in the top half of Figure 6–6. At the same time, few Mondale voters wanted to see increases in spending for the military. As the lower portion of the figure reveals, the public accurately perceived the two candidates as having distinctly different positions on future defense spending. Furthermore, most supporters of both candidates had a moderate position on this issue; at the same time, they perceived the candidates as holding rather extreme positions.

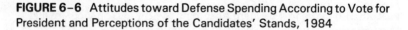

FIGURE 6-6 Attitudes toward Defense Spending According to Vote for President and Perceptions of the Candidates' Stands, 1984

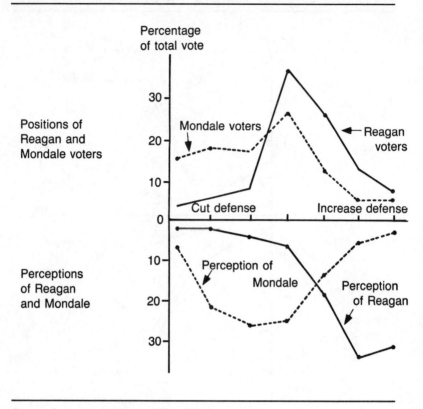

Source: Center for Political Studies 1984 National Election Study.

A similar pattern is shown in Figure 6–7 on a major domestic issue, the choice between cutting government services or maintaining them at current levels. Very few of Reagan's voters were in favor of maintaining services at current levels, and even fewer of Mondale's supporters thought services should be cut. Again, Reagan and Mondale were perceived as offering distinctly different policy choices on government services.

Although issue positions were definitely related to presidential vote choice in 1984, these relationships are not especially strong. It has been suggested that the lack of a strong relationship between an individual's issue positions and his or her vote choice results from the fact that the analyst chooses the issues for analysis, issues that are not

FIGURE 6-7 Attitudes toward Cutting or Maintaining Government Services According to Vote for President and Perceptions of Candidates' Stands, 1984

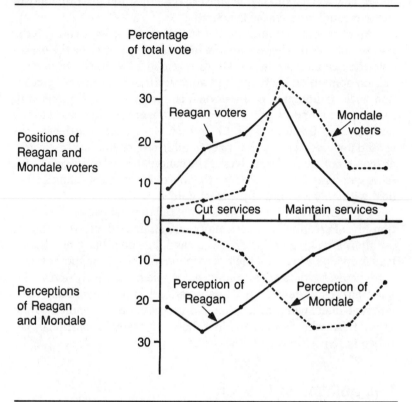

Percentage of total vote

Positions of Reagan and Mondale voters

Perceptions of Reagan and Mondale

Source: Center for Political Studies 1984 National Election Study.

necessarily important to the individual. If the voter is allowed to define what he or she sees as the most important issue, a somewhat stronger relationship between his or her position on issues and voting decisions is found.[8]

Others have argued that a rational and issue-oriented voter judges the past performance of the candidates rather than simply comparing

[8]David RePass, "Issue Salience and Party Choice," *American Political Science Review* 65 (June 1971): 368–400.

the candidates' promises for the future.[9] For example, in 1980, Carter was widely perceived as unable to govern effectively and, for many voters, this was a more salient concern than their relative proximity to the two candidates on the issues.

Another serious matter for the analyst studying issue voting is the number of voters who are unable to locate themselves or the candidates on one or more issues. Of all voters in 1972, about 10 percent had no opinion on Vietnam, and another 10 percent had no perception of the candidates' positions on Vietnam. In 1984, 17 percent of the electorate had no opinions on government spending and cutting services, and an additional 10 percent were unable to locate the candidates' positions on the issue. Similar proportions of the electorate could not locate themselves or the candidates on the subject of defense spending. Thus analyses of the role of issues in vote choice often deal with only a subset of the electorate.

Furthermore, this analysis does not tell us what causes these relationships. Perception of issues may cause an individual's vote choice, or, alternatively, a preference for a candidate on other grounds may lead individuals to adjust their perceptions of issues in support of their vote choice. No data are available that would conclusively resolve this question. Regardless of the causal relationship, it is significant that, although many voters lack opinions on issues or on the candidates' position, those who do have opinions show considerable consistency between issue positions and vote choice.

Determinants of Vote Choice

The preceding sections have considered candidate images, party images, and issues as short-term forces that either reinforce or deflect voters from their long-term party loyalty. An interesting, but far more difficult, question is the relative impact of these various factors on vote choice. Since all of these factors are strongly interrelated and almost certainly all influence each other, it is virtually impossible to untangle their effects with the kind of data available in nationwide surveys. If one assumes that issues are all-important in determining vote choice, most voting behavior can be accounted for by issues alone, ignoring other factors. On the other hand, to assume that party identi-

---

[9]Morris Fiorina, *Retrospective Voting in American National Elections* (New Haven, Conn.: Yale University Press, 1981).

fication and a few social characteristics are all-important accounts for most voting behavior with these variables, ignoring issues. The conflicting conclusions that are reached are largely a matter of the theoretical assumptions with which one starts.

A careful assessment of issue voting in comparison with party loyalty was presented by Nie, Verba, and Petrocik in *The Changing American Voter*.[10] The results of their analysis for presidential elec-

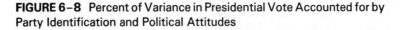

FIGURE 6-8 Percent of Variance in Presidential Vote Accounted for by Party Identification and Political Attitudes

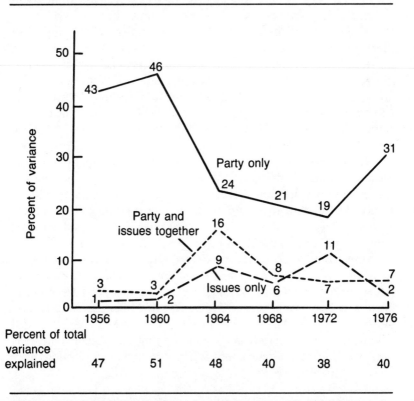

Source: Norman H. Nie, Sidney Verba, and John R. Petrocik, *The Changing American Voter* (Cambridge, Mass.: Harvard University Press, 1976), Figure 16.8, p. 304. Reprinted by permission. The 1976 entries were estimated from John R. Petrocik, "Contextual Sources of Voting Behavior: The Changeable American Voter," in John C. Pierce and John L. Sullivan (eds.), *The Electorate Reconsidered* (Beverly Hills, Calif.: Sage Publications, 1980), Figure 13.4, p. 269.

[10]Nie, Verba, and Petrocik, *The Changing American Voter*, chap. 16.

tions from 1956 to 1972, presented in Figure 6–8 along with a 1976 update by Petrocik, reveal a rather dramatic change in the pattern in 1964. There was a relatively sharp drop in the impact of party loyalty (independent of issues) in 1964 and the following elections. Issues have never been as important as party in determining vote choice, but their influence increased from 1964 until 1976 when the earlier pattern returned. The joint impact of party and issues, that is, the influence of two factors that cannot be separated statistically, has also increased in recent elections. It is extremely difficult to measure issues for this purpose, and analysts have not agreed on how to do it. There are various assessments of the impact of party and issues on presidential vote choice, but most findings are similar to Figure 6–8.

In the light of these difficulties, some analysis of the impact of short-term forces has focused on the unique impact of each element in the presence of others. One of the best examples of this mode of analysis is Donald Stokes's effort to measure attitudinal forces influencing presidential vote choices.[11] Following Stokes's method, Arthur Miller and Martin Wattenberg have analyzed the eight presidential elections from 1952 to 1984;[12] their results are shown in Table 6–1. Negative values indicate a factor that helped the Democratic candidate; positive values indicate a benefit to the Republican candidate. The perception of group benefits is a consistently large pro-Democratic element in all nine elections. Foreign policy matters have almost always helped the Republican candidate, with the exception of Goldwater in 1964 and Reagan in 1984. The impact of foreign affairs and domestic policies was unusually strong and pro-Republican in 1980. This reflected the strongly unfavorable reactions to Carter's handling of the economy and the Iranian hostage crisis. In contrast, the candidates' personalities had an unusually weak influence on vote choice in 1980. The evidence presented by Shanks and Miller also suggests that personalities played a small role in voting for president in that year.[13]

Although Ronald Reagan was the winning candidate in both 1980 and 1984, the factors determining his success in the two elections were

---

[11]Angus Campbell et al., *The American Voter* (New York: John Wiley & Sons, 1960), pp. 524–531.

[12]Arthur H. Miller and Martin P. Wattenberg, "Policy and Performance Voting in the 1980 Election," paper presented at the American Political Science Association meeting, 1981, cited in Niemi and Weisberg, *Controversies in Voting Behavior*, 2nd ed. (Washington, D.C.: CQ Press, 1984), p. 91.

[13]Shanks and Miller, "Policy Direction and Performance Evaluation: Complementary Explanations of the Reagan Elections."

TABLE 6–1 Net Impact of Six Attitudinal Components in Determining Vote Choice, 1952–1984

	1952	1956	1960	1964	1968	1972	1976	1980	1984
Domestic policy	-1.3	-0.9	-0.5	-2.4	1.1	1.4	-0.7	3.1	1.5
Foreign policy	3.3	2.5	1.8	-0.3	1.0	3.2	0.4	2.8	-0.3
Party management	5.4	1.2	1.2	-0.3	1.5	0.0	0.2	0.6	0.5
Group benefits	-4.3	-5.5	-4.0	-2.6	-3.6	-4.6	-4.5	-4.5	-5.6
Democratic candidate	-1.2	0.2	-2.0	-4.0	0.9	4.3	-0.1	-0.4	1.3
Republican candidate	4.4	7.6	5.7	-2.6	1.6	4.0	2.2	-0.5	1.5

Note: Positive values are pro-Republican effects; negative values indicate a Democratic advantage. The values can be interpreted as the percentage of the vote moved in one partisan direction or the other.

Source: Arthur H. Miller and Martin P. Wattenberg, "Policy and Performance Voting in the 1980 Election," cited in Richard Niemi and Herbert Weisberg (eds.), *Controversies in Voting Behavior,* 2nd ed. (Washington, D.C.: Congressional Quarterly, 1984), p. 91; 1984 data provided by Martin P. Wattenberg.

not the same. In 1984, both foreign and domestic policy considerations had declined in importance as can be seen in Table 6–1. The personalities of the candidates, on the other hand, had become significant pro-Republican factors.

During the conventions and the brief period of the campaign, political parties cannot do much about the basic partisan strength of each side; therefore, they concentrate on presenting candidate images and issue positions calculated to have greatest appeal to the uncommitted voters. Even if the outcome of an election is not substantially affected by party strategies, the content of the campaign and the meaning the election comes to have for leaders and the public are created by these strategies. The information in Table 6–1 can be viewed as measures of the content of the campaign and its meaning for voters.

Meaning of an Election

Politicians and news commentators spend much time and energy interpreting and explaining the outcome of an election. The difficulties in assigning meaning to election results are easy to exaggerate; the most important element is usually quite clear—the winner. Elections are primarily a mechanism for selecting certain governmental leaders and, just as important, for removing leaders from office and preventing others from gaining office. Nevertheless, an effort is often made to discover the policy implications of patterns of voting and to read meaning into the outcome of elections. This effort raises two problems for analysis: first, the policy implications of the winning and losing candidates' issues stands and, second, the issue content of the voters' decisions.

In both 1980 and 1984, Ronald Reagan articulated an unusually clear set of ideological and policy alternatives. Not all elections offer voters a clear choice between a conservative and a liberal candidate, but the 1980 and 1984 races between Reagan and Carter and Reagan and Mondale were widely perceived as doing so. Since Reagan won both elections by wide margins, his administration understandably claimed a popular mandate for a wide range of policies.

It is perfectly appropriate to attribute policy significance to an election on the basis of the policy preferences of the winning candidates, so long as it is not implied that the voters had these policy implications in mind when they voted. That is, it is appropriate to observe that the election outcome means lower taxes or an expanded program because the victor has pledged to implement lower taxes or to expand a program. But it is very difficult to establish that the voters' preferences have certain policy meaning or that the votes for a particular candidate provide a policy mandate. Several obstacles lie in the way of stating simply what policies are implied by the behavior of the voters. In many elections, the voters are unaware of the stands of candidates on issues, and sometimes the voters are mistaken in their perceptions of candidates' stands.

Furthermore, many voters are not concerned with issues as such in a campaign, but vote according to their party loyalty or a candidate's personality. Their vote has no particular policy significance but reflects a general preference for one candidate. Voters who supported Reagan had an unfavorable view of Carter's performance as president, especially his handling of the hostage crisis. The dissatisfaction with Carter was clear enough; however, the expectations about Reagan were quite vague and perhaps limited to the hope that he would strengthen national defense and balance the budget. By 1984, President Reagan enjoyed favorable ratings and he benefited from the unpopularity of the Mondale-Ferraro ticket. To the extent that members of the electorate were aware of specific policies of the Reagan administration, they held mixed views but by no means wholeheartedly endorsed these policies. As in 1980, President Reagan was elected to some extent in spite of his positions on major issues.

A candidate has considerable freedom under most circumstances to interpret a victory with respect to the issues. Obviously, President Reagan felt free to interpret his mandate as requiring a massive tax cut but not dictating a balanced budget. There was no more basis for this distinction in public opinion than a mandate to reduce social programs drastically. Most election outcomes are just this vague and conflicting with respect to most issues. This partially explains the failure of the American political system to impose policy stands on elected officials. This illustrates as well the opportunities for leadership afforded to electoral victors. If they are perceived as successful in handling their job, political leaders can convert their following to support their policies, and subsequently it will appear as if the public had demanded the policies in the first place.

On the other hand, it is also true that the supporters of a candidate usually do not intensely or widely oppose his or her stands. Voters will often vote for candidates who hold views they do not share, but these views are on matters of little interest to the voters. Presumably, voters seldom support candidates who hold views with which they disagree intensely.

American elections are hardly a classic model of democracy with rational, well-informed voters making dispassionate decisions. On the other hand, American elections provide an acceptable opportunity for parties and candidates to attempt to win or hold public office. Although the electorate is capable upon occasion of responding to issue appeals both positively and negatively, the electorate does not appear easily moved by most appeals. The electorate offers the parties modest opportunities to gain voters without offering extreme temptations to reckless appeals.

7

Political Communication and Campaigns

$$\star\;\star\;\star$$

Much attention has been focused on the process of change in political opinions, both in terms of the conditions for such change and the possibilities of instigating widespread changes in political beliefs through the mass media. At the extremes, the process of influencing political opinions is labeled *brainwashing* or *propaganda;* but really only a matter of degree and normative judgment separates these forms of influence from political persuasion, campaigning, or even education. All the efforts covered by these terms are directed toward changing individuals' political ideas, values, and opinions or toward fostering some political action. Enormous amounts of time and money are expended in American society to change political views. The very diversity of these efforts to influence the public mind, along with the diversity and complexity of the society itself, makes highly unlikely a quick or uniform public response to any one of these attempts.

Political persuasion probably is most effective in casual personal relationships. The impact of the mass media is probably important in shaping the contours of political discourse, but only gradually and over fairly long periods of time. At the same time, the role that the media have in making information widely available is extremely important in creating the conditions under which attitude change occurs. This chapter will consider the basic processes of opinion change and the impact of the mass media and election campaigns on individual political behavior.

Functions of Opinions for Individuals

Social psychology suggests that an individual's opinions can serve various purposes: cognitive, social, and psychological. Cognitive functions of opinions cover the efforts to give meaning to our social environment and to relate elements of belief and knowledge to one another. Opinions generally relate directly or indirectly to an individual's most significant goals or values. And somehow the policy supported by a political opinion is expected to be consistent with one's most important political values.

Opinions serve a social function if they aid the individual in adjusting to others or in becoming part of a group. In some cases individuals may use opinions to set themselves apart from others. Political and social issues may be too unimportant generally to serve social purposes for most people, and there is little evidence to indicate strong social conformity pressures on most political issues. Nevertheless, for highly salient issues an individual is apt to find that holding a socially unacceptable view is both uncomfortable and costly.

An opinion also may serve purposes for an individual that are not dependent on its social, economic, or political meaning but, rather, on its special psychological significance for the individual. For example, an individual might hold opinions strongly prejudicial against some group because it enhances self-esteem to feel superior to some others, or an individual might imagine that some group has undesirable qualities of which the person rids himself or herself by projecting those qualities on the group. The danger or disadvantage of psychological attachments of this kind is that the opinions so based are not responsive to ordinary influence because of their psychological importance to the individual. Most Americans do not appear to attach strong psychological meaning to their political opinions. Furthermore, in a modern pluralistic society with its open political processes, opinions on significant political subjects are unlikely to remain privatized and solely of psychological relevance to the individual; opinions also take on social and cognitive functions.

Most discussions of political opinions imply a more or less reasoned handling of opinions by individuals: that individuals intelligently relate their opinions to one another and that a logical relation exists between a goal and a preference for policies leading to that goal. The implication of this perspective, as we shall see in the next section, is that opinions can be changed if the cognitive content of the attitude is changed, that is, if new information is brought to the attention of the individual. While this is a useful point of view, it is necessary to be aware that if individuals hold their opinions for the social or psychological purposes they serve, rather than for the cognitive, providing the individuals with more information or altering the policy implications of the opinion will not necessarily lead to opinion change.

Opinion Consistency and Dissonance

The analysis of inconsistency in opinions has much in common with the cross-pressure thesis considered in Chapter 3. In psychology this analysis of opinions has taken the form of identifying elements of several opinions as consistent with one another or as being in conflict (dissonant). Because dissonance is assumed to be disturbing, an individual presumably will try to avoid or to reduce dissonance. An example of dissonance should clarify these concepts.[1]

Suppose a Republican believes that all Democratic administrations are corrupt and that Republicans stand for honest government, and the individual's party loyalty is justified on this basis. If the individual becomes aware of information that suggests a Republican governor is taking bribes, this conflicts with the person's earlier views and may create dissonance among them. The dissonance could be reduced by justifying his or her loyalty on a new basis or by denying or discrediting the new information. A denial might take the form of deciding that the governor is being framed by opponents.

Individuals have many psychological defenses against the potential dissonance represented by new information that conflicts with their existing attitudes: *selective exposure*, or not paying attention to conflicting information; *selective perception*, the misinterpretation of such information; rejecting the source of the information as lacking credibility; *compartmentalization*, that is, not making the connec-

---

[1]The classic statement on cognitive dissonance is Leon Festinger, *A Theory of Cognitive Dissonance* (Evanston, Ill.: Row, Peterson, 1957). For some of the most interesting experimental work in this field, see Milton J. Rosenberg et al., *Attitude Organization and Change* (New Haven, Conn.: Yale University Press, 1960).

tions between dissonant attitudes; and *rationalization*, the unwarranted reinterpretation of the connections between attitudes in order to remove dissonance. Should the meaning of the information be unavoidable, attitude change to restore harmony may result. Typically, individuals will change dissonant patterns in the easiest way; the opinions or beliefs that are least important to the individual will be changed rather than salient, important ideas or values.

Political opinions are probably most often changed simply by providing individuals with more information. This additional information may be no more than some new facts about the environment or indications that many political leaders whom an individual respects hold a particular view. The low salience of most political issues, plus the widespread emphasis on debate and discussion, leads to circumstances that improve the opportunities for changing opinions with information.

Political Communication

Individuals in the public receive ideas and information intended to alter their political opinions from a variety of sources. Some sources are political leaders and commentators whose views arrive impersonally through the mass media; others are friends, co-workers, and family members who influence opinions through personal contact. Much remains to be learned about political persuasion and communication, but at least occasionally many Americans engage in attempts to influence others, and almost everyone is regularly the recipient of large quantities of political communication.

A somewhat oversimplified view of the transmission of political information would have the media beaming a uniform message to a mass audience made up of isolated individuals. The audience would receive all or most of its information from the media; thus, public opinion would be a direct product of the information and perspective provided through the media. A more complex view suggests that information is transmitted in what is called a "two-step flow of communication."[2] Information is transmitted from "opinion elites" (leaders in the society like politicians, organizational leaders, news commen-

---

[2]Elihu Katz and Paul F. Lazarsfeld, *Personal Influence: The Part Played by People in the Flow of Mass Communications* (New York: The Free Press, 1964).

tators) to a minority of the public, "opinion leaders," and from them to the remainder of the public:

Opinion Elites

Opinion Leaders

Public

The information from opinion elites usually is sent through the mass media, but this view implies that only a portion of the audience, the opinion leaders, is attentive to any particular type of information such as political news. These intermediaries, the opinion leaders, then interpret, modify, and explain facts and events to their friends and neighbors who are less interested in or concerned with these happenings. In the process, the original message conveyed through the media becomes many somewhat different messages as it reaches the public.

The two-step flow model may not be literally true in most cases, and public opinion research has generally failed to turn up many people who recognize themselves as opinion leaders. Even so, most members of the public probably do receive information from the mass media in the context of their social groups. Thus, they filter the information and interpretations of the media through not only their own perceptions, experiences, and existing attitudes but also those of people around them. Only when the media have the attention of most members of the audience and a virtual monopoly over the kinds of information received by a public that has few existing attitudes about the subject can the media produce anything like a uniform change in public attitudes. As was noted in Chapter 6 in reference to the manipulation of candidate images, these circumstances are rare in American society.

Speculation on the nature of political communication has ranged from alarm over the vulnerability of the mass public to manipulation through the media, to annoyance at the difficulty of reaching the public. The American people make use of the mass media to inform themselves on matters of interest, but this does not mean that the public pays attention to everything in the media. Individuals have a remarkable ability to ignore information, a capacity as fully developed as the ability to absorb information. Influencing individuals on a subject about which they feel strongly is extremely difficult because they reject the media content, and influencing individuals on a subject to which they are indifferent offers problems because they ignore the media content.

Also, the media are difficult to use for manipulation because so many different points of view are found there. An extremely wide range of political perspectives is available to some degree in the mass media, although some perspectives are much more frequently available and more persuasively presented than others. The media in American society allow all views to enjoy some expression, although media coverage of many topics may be expressed in a manner extremely favorable to some viewpoints and unfavorable to others. It would be extremely difficult to disentangle the bias associated with the news and commentary in the media from the distortion found in the individual's reception of political information. The public has a considerable capacity for ignoring media content or misinterpreting that content. Either of these conditions would be adequate to account for considerable discrepancy between political reality and the public image of that reality. No analyst of public opinion would contend that the American people are extremely well informed politically or hold views that are free of systematic bias. There is, however, quite a difference between this recognition and the contention that the mass media cause particular misperceptions. On the other hand, the long-term impact of the biases and style of the mass-communication channels on public attitudes has not received adequate attention. Universal exposure to the prevailing political culture as offered through the mass media in news reporting, popular commentary, and the arts will certainly make subcultural variations more difficult to establish and maintain.

Television often plays a critical role in bringing events and issues, like the Vietnam War and the Watergate scandals, to the American public. Without television, the basic information about Vietnam and Watergate would have reached the public, but television appears to have presented certain types of information in an exceptionally dramatic or impressive way.

The taking of American hostages in Iran and the daily television coverage of demonstrations there greatly heightened the emotional impact of that episode on the American public. Without television, the takeover of the American embassy in Teheran would have been a serious international incident. With the regular presentation of fear and grief on television, millions of Americans were also deeply touched by the experience of the hostages and their families. Without a doubt, the continuous media attention focused on the hostage crisis limited the options available to American decision makers. They could not hold out and wait for an opportune time to negotiate after the public had lost interest; the presence of the media may well have affected the course of events. In similar fashion, President Reagan's policy for Lebanon was practically determined and withdrawal almost assured by the strong public reaction to television coverage of the bombing of the Marine barracks at the Beirut airport.

In contrast, the Reagan administration limited the power of the press generally and television in particular by imposing a news blackout on the Grenada invasion in 1983. For some time only an official version of events was available; the confusion, the accidents, the military oddity of the episode were all concealed from public view during the period when Grenada was a major news item. For what might be called public relations reasons, the Reagan administration did not want critical, conflicting news reports contradicting the positive, official story. Journalists were dismayed that the public seemingly approved of this interference with free press coverage. Although the public is undoubtedly influenced by the critical commentary in a free press or the news coverage on television—we could say that the public benefits from this freedom—it is not necessarily the case that a majority of the public welcomes criticism or is grateful to the bearer of bad news.

There is much discussion in the scholarly literature on mass media of the capacity to bring matters to the attention of the public or to conceal them.[3] Usually this is called *agenda setting* and suggests the media have great influence over what the public is aware of and concerned with.

It is certainly true that many items of potential news are not reported either in the print media or on television, a process often referred to as *gate keeping*.[4] The media are more selective than a phrase like "all the news that's fit to print" suggests. The idea of agenda setting is that items are kept from the public that would have been of considerable interest or that items are made to seem important which the public otherwise would ignore. Neither of these effects is easily demonstrated with political information and opinions. It is fairly easy to show that a particular newspaper or a given television station may

---

[3]For an early statement of this point, see Bernard C. Cohen, *The Press and Foreign Policy* (Princeton, N.J.: Princeton Unversity Press, 1963).

[4]See Everette E. Dennis, *The Media Society* (Dubuque, Iowa: Wm. C. Brown, 1978), chaps. 5, 7.

ignore certain topics or exaggerate others, but it is extremely difficult to find evidence of any impact of selective coverage on the public.

Political Campaigns

Some efforts to influence political views are sufficiently organized and elaborate to be described as *campaigns.* And, of course, election campaigns are the most prominent among these. Election campaigns have several purposes: (1) to publicize the attractive qualities of candidates, platforms, and performance; (2) to raise money and to recruit workers for the campaign; and (3) to increase turnout for candidates or a referendum, the ultimate test of a successful campaign. To some degree, modern election campaigns involve two quite distinct assaults on the voter, one through the mass media and the other through the more localized and personalized activities of party workers. In the remainder of this chapter, the extent of campaign participation and the impact of personal contact will be examined as well as the impact of the mass media in election campaigns. Finally, the overall impact of election campaigns will be considered in terms of their influence on the voting choices of the electorate.

Campaign Participation and Its Impact

The greatest spectacle of American politics, the presidential campaign and election, involves millions of workers in telephoning, doorbell ringing, addressing envelopes, and doing the work of the campaign. A rather small proportion of American citizens is attracted to campaign work, considering the crucial role of elections in our political system. As Table 7–1 shows, the percent of campaign workers did not change much during the period from 1952 to 1984. Even though there is considerable overlap among individuals in each category, the percentages do not represent the same set of individuals. For example, many individuals who contribute financially are not involved in the campaign in any other way. More than half of the members of political clubs and organizations are not currently involved in any campaign activity. When all forms of campaign activity are counted, well over 10 percent of the electorate is involved in some way.

Campaign activity has generally been greater among Republicans than among Democrats or independents during this thirty-two-year period. In 1964, a large proportion of strongly partisan Republi-

TABLE 7-1 Campaign Activities in Presidential Election Years, 1952–1984

	1952	1956	1960	1964	1968	1972	1976	1980	1984
Do you belong to any political club or organization?	2%	3%	3%	4%	3%	a	a	3%	a
Did you give any money or buy tickets or anything to help the campaign for one of the parties or candidates?	4%	10%	11%	11%	12%	10%	9% 8%[b]	8% 5%[c]	7% 5%[c]
Did you go to any political meetings, rallies, dinners, or things like that?	7%	7%	8%	8%	14%	9%	6%	8%	4%
Did you do any other work for one of the parties or candidates?	3%	3%	5%	5%	5%	5%	4%	4%	4%

[a]This question was not asked in 1972, 1976 and 1984.
[b]Percent mentioning a tax check-off contribution.
[c]Percent giving to political groups during the campaign, but not to parties or candidates.
Source: Survey Research Center/Center for Political Studies National Election Studies.

cans were giving money (about one-third) and attending meetings or rallies (about one-quarter), whereas among Democrats, independents, and less partisan Republicans, less than one-tenth were active in these ways. By 1984, the level of campaign activity among Republicans had diminished somewhat, although the Republicans usually have an edge over Democrats. Over the years, active independents have worked disproportionately for the Republican Party; even so, Democrats have about as many active campaigners as the Republicans, since there are more Democrats from which campaigners can be drawn. In 1984, Republicans were somewhat more active than Democrats, undoubtedly reflecting the different levels of enthusiasm in the campaign.

Only in making campaign contributions do strongly partisan Republicans remain distinctively different, with one in ten of them contributing to their party. In part this difference is a result of the higher socioeconomic position of Republicans since campaign contributions come disproportionately from the well-to-do. Not only can high-income individuals better afford to give, but they are also easier to locate for solicitation. The Republican party's advantage in campaign activity shows up most clearly in fund raising. Leaving aside the rather notorious efforts at fund raising by the Committee to Reelect the President in 1972, the Republican party regularly has been able to raise more money through campaign solicitation than has the Democratic party.

Recently, campaign financing has been revolutionized by technological advances in direct mail solicitation. Working from huge mailing lists stored in computers, campaign organizations or, more likely, special interest Political Action Committees, can efficiently send appeals to large numbers of potential contributors. Since the lists are developed from membership lists of organizations supporting various causes or from subscription lists of periodicals with particular points of view, the appeals can be tailored to the interests and ideology of the recipients. Even if the solicitation does not elicit a contribution, the message on which the appeal is based will get into the hands of a potential supporter. Initially, conservative organizations used this form of fund raising and voter contact more extensively but, increasingly, liberal interest groups are adopting the same technology.

One of the most direct attempts to influence voters is door-to-door solicitation and telephoning. The reported impact of these efforts by party workers to influence voters through personal contact is not impressive. Almost all voters report that they have not been influenced in their vote choice by party contacts. By 1984, a large share of this contact was by telephone and not necessarily as effective as face-to-face contact. However, party contact may influence turnout and the level of financial contributions to the party. Since 1952, the proportion of the electorate reporting that it has been contacted personally by one or both parties has increased—from 11 percent in 1952 to 17 percent in 1956 to 20 percent in 1960 to 26 percent in 1964. Personal contact remained at this level through 1980. During the 1984 campaign, personal contact declined somewhat to 20 percent although there appeared to be more frequent contacts with a smaller number of voters. The number of voters contacted—about twenty-five million voters in 1984—represents an enormous effort by party organizations. Whether it has much impact or not, contacting people is an activity that political organizations without great wealth can perform; and since some evidence of payoff exists, it is an activity not likely to be abandoned.

Mass Media and Election Campaigns

At least as important as personal party contact during an election campaign is the contact made by candidates and party leaders through the mass media, mainly newspaper, radio, and television. The attempts to communicate with the American public on political matters face an awkward dilemma. The attentive members of the public, the individuals most likely to receive political messages, are least likely to be influenced by one or a few items of information. On the other hand, the individuals who are open to persuasion are also uninterested in politics and not likely to pay attention to politics in the media.

In assessing the impact of the mass media on political behavior, it is useful to draw some distinctions that are not always made. First, the impact of information may be different depending on the type of media through which it is received. Precisely the same information received through television, radio, or a newspaper may impress the recipient quite differently. For example, viewing a television picture of a speech may be more dramatic than hearing it on radio or reading the text in a newspaper. Something like this occurred in 1960 when television viewers of the first of three debates between Kennedy and Nixon had a more unfavorable impression of Nixon than radio listeners. On the other hand, a difficult topic may be more easily absorbed by reading and rereading a newspaper article in contrast to having the story flash by once on television.

Second, the media differ in what they offer. Simple elements of information are more quickly and dramatically presented to a large audience on television than through the print media. Television, however, may systematically underinform its audience by rarely offering more than a minute or two on one story. The more the public wants information and is motivated to seek it, the more important newspapers become. It is easy to search for items of information in newspapers, quite difficult with radio and television. The characteristics of the media give them different roles in the formation of public opinion. Generally, television alerts the public to a variety of topics; newspapers inform the public in greater depth on a few topics.

Third, the impact of political advertising in the several media should be treated differently from other elements. The growth of television advertising has changed campaign financing drastically, although it has been difficult to establish an impact on vote choice that justifies the investment in television advertising. The major impact of television advertising as well as other campaign activities appears to be increasing voters' awareness of the issue stands of the candidates —mainly after the voters have made up their minds on a preferred candidate. A study by Patterson and McClure in the Syracuse, New York, area in 1972 attempted to assess the relative impact of television news versus television political advertising on voters' perceptions of the candidates.[5] They concluded that television advertising contained more explicit information about the candidates' stands on issues than did news stories and had a correspondingly greater impact on voters' awareness of the issue positions of candidates. Television news stories were too brief and focused too much on campaign action to convey much issue information to the viewer. The impact of political advertising on TV was greatest among voters with less exposure to other news sources. For those more attentive to the mass media in general, newspapers were the greatest source of political information.

Fourth, the impact of editorial endorsements by newspapers (television and radio stations rarely make endorsements) should be assessed independently of news coverage, although editorial preferences may bias news stories. Newspaper endorsements seemingly have

---

[5]Thomas E. Patterson and Robert D. McClure, "Television News and Televised Political Advertising: Their Impact on the Voter," paper presented at the National Conference on Money and Politics, Washington, D.C., 1974; and Thomas E. Patterson and Robert D. McClure, *Political Advertising: Voter Reaction to Televised Political Commercials* (Princeton, N.J.: Citizens' Research Foundation, 1973).

a minimal impact in presidential elections where many other sources of influence exist.[6] In less salient races at the local level, a newspaper editorial may influence many voters.[7] Some concern exists that major newspaper chains could wield significant power nationally by lining up their papers behind one candidate. In recent years the large chains have left their papers free to make decisions locally, and while this might change at any time, the impact on a national election might not even be discernible.

Finally, there is the impact of news and news commentary available from the mass media. Almost all attention has focused on the impact of television and most assessments consider its impact over brief periods. Any effects that develop over a long time would be difficult to disentangle from other influences. We can demonstrate a considerable impact of certain news items when attitudes are not well formed or strongly held. For example, Patterson reports data showing that in 1976 the initial public reaction to the second TV debate between Ford and Carter was favorable to Ford. As news commentary, especially on television, emphasized a mistaken statement by President Ford about the absence of communist domination in Eastern Europe, public opinion shifted to see Carter as the winner. In the course of two days, public evaluation shifted from 53 percent to 35 percent in favor of Ford to 58 percent to 29 percent in favor of Carter.[8] Without arguing that the public's opinion on who won the debate had any special consequences, it must be conceded that this represents an impressive instance of media influence over public opinion.

Obviously, in order for the media to have an impact on an individual's political attitudes and behavior, the individual must give some degree of attention to the media when political information is being conveyed. Almost all Americans have access to television and watch political news at least some of the time. A majority of Americans read a daily newspaper for political news. There is the general expectation that the most interested citizens are most attentive to political news and that strong partisans will follow the media more closely than weaker partisans or independents.

In 1976, Thomas Patterson found a strong relationship between political interest and media attention. He collected extensive data on

[6]Dennis, *The Media Society*, pp. 37–41.

[7]Michael B. MacKuen and Steven L. Coombs, *More than News* (Beverly Hills, Calif.: Sage Publications, 1981).

[8]Thomas E. Patterson, *The Mass Media Election* (New York: Praeger, 1980), pp. 123, 125.

samples of adults in Erie, Pennsylvania, and Los Angeles during the primary and general election campaign.[9] This is an unusual collection of data among public opinion studies because it focuses explicitly on media behavior. Patterson's analysis, reported mainly in *The Mass Media Election*, permits a distinction between reported media attention and the ability to recall political information from the media. Both attention to and recall of political news either on television or in a newspaper is greatest among the highly interested. In this most interested group there is some overlap between careful attention to television and newspapers, but in the rest of the public very few people are making great use of both media.

Patterson has reported that newspapers are more extensively used as a souce of information than television.[10] By the end of the 1976 campaign, 22 percent of Patterson's respondents could recall a newspaper story with some accuracy and 15 percent could recall a television news item with comparable accuracy. Earlier in the year during the primary elections, neither television nor newspaper users could recall political stories with great accuracy.

The way in which partisans use the media varies with political characteristics. Democrats make less effective use of both television and newspapers than Republicans in that they seem to retain less information from their exposure to the media. Independents are less attentive than either group of partisans. Strong Republicans contrast with strong Democrats in that they depend heavily on newspapers—more than any other partisan grouping—and very little on television. Strong Democrats use both media equally and depend more on television than other partisans and independents.

The impact of mass media exposure on voting behavior in earlier elections was studied by Philip Converse[11] of the Center for Political Studies, who drew several conclusions based on findings like those represented in Figure 7-1. The voters most stable in their preferences (whether stability is measured during a campaign or between elections) would be those who are highly attentive to mass media but firmly committed, and those who pay no attention to media communication and remain stable in their vote choice because no new infor-

---

[9]See ibid., pp. 14–15. Five major interviews and two brief supplemental surveys were done for the two panels beginning in February.

[10]Ibid., especially chap. 6.

[11]Philip Converse, "Information Flow and the Stability of Partisan Attitudes," *Public Opinion Quarterly* 26 (Winter 1962): 578–599.

FIGURE 7-1 The Hypothetical Relationship between Mass Media Attention and Stability of Voting Behavior

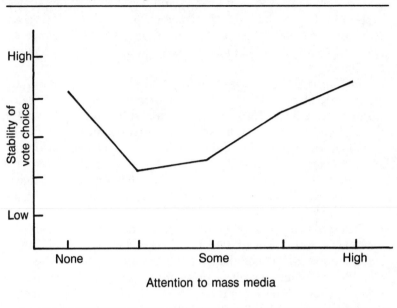

mation is introduced to change their vote. The shifting, unstable voters are more likely to have moderate exposure to mass media. The reasoning behind this expected relationship is quite compelling; unfortunately efforts at replicating Converse's findings for other election years have failed to uncover similar patterns. One difficulty may be the virtual disappearance of voters with no exposure to the mass media in recent years.

Overall, research has shown little individual change in vote choice or issue positions during campaigns, and these consistent findings have led to the generalization that media campaigns have little effect. We have mentioned at several points that there is rarely evidence of much vote-switching during a campaign. To some degree this is because studies have devoted most attention to highly salient general elections—the types of elections in which voters are most likely to have made up their minds early and firmly. On the other hand, prior to the general election campaign, the public's choices appear volatile even between well-known candidates. In the summer of 1979, Democrats preferred Kennedy over Carter three to one as their party's nominee for president.[12] By the end of the year, they were even, and by March 1980, Carter was ahead of Kennedy two to one among Democrats. Between January and March in 1980, Republican support for Reagan shifted from 45 percent to 32 percent and back to 56 percent.[13] Nothing comparable to this magnitude of change was observed between the nominating conventions and the election in November.

Similar volatility was seen during 1983 when public opinion polls consistently showed Walter Mondale running ahead of President Reagan in trial heats. Early in 1984, their positions reversed so that by the beginning of the presidential primaries Mondale trailed Reagan by about ten percentage points. This change cannot be directly attributed to media coverage of political events, but the change does coincide with more and more media attention to criticism of Mondale—much of it by fellow Democrats competing with him in the primaries.

There is a great deal of political learning during a campaign. Voters become aware of candidates they had never heard of and gain an impression of these candidates' stands on issues. Even well-known candidates like an incumbent president may not have a clearly defined set of issue positions in the public's view before the campaign.

In studying the 1976 election, Patterson found that the association between voters' issue positions and their candidate choices increased over the course of the campaign.[14] Voters in that sample did not appear to be persuaded to change their attitudes on issues by candidate appeals or to switch their vote choices; rather, as they learned which positions the candidates took, they discovered (in many instances) that they were closer to their preferred candidate. This finding might be used to argue that the campaign is a process of clarification, an articulation of issue linkages that were potential all along.

It is often imagined that considerable polarization occurs during a campaign. The evidence for this is uneven. There is a slight tendency for weak partisans to become strong partisans during the last months of a campaign. But there is no similar evidence that the public takes more extreme positions on issues as the campaign progresses. They do,

---

[12]*Gallup Opinion Index*, Report No. 183, December 1980, p. 51.

[13]"Opinion Roundup," *Public Opinion* 3 (April/May 1980): 38.

[14]Thomas E. Patterson, "Vote Choice in the 1976 Presidential Primary Elections," paper presented at the annual meeting of the Southern Political Science Association, New Orleans, 1977.

however, perceive the candidates' positions as more extreme by the end of the campaign. In the 1980 election, one that might reasonably have been described as polarizing, the public viewed Carter and Reagan as further apart at the end of the campaign than at the beginning. During this same period, the public moved away from extreme liberal and conservative views and toward the middle. Public opinion becomes more orderly during a campaign. The relationship between party or ideology and various issues strengthens somewhat during a campaign, although the change is not great.

In social science a most important generalization about media attention has to do with *selective exposure.* Selective exposure refers to a tendency to select information that conforms to one's ideas and values. Individuals allegedly avoid media content that would conflict with their present point of view and seek out information that reinforces their views. For example, Patterson and McClure found that Democrats who planned to vote for Nixon were particularly attentive to television commercials critical of McGovern that were offered by "Democrats for Nixon."[15] In the terms used above, an individual selects mass-media content in order to avoid or reduce dissonance. It is persuasive to argue that Democrats are more likely than Republicans to read news stories about Democratic candidates or to watch a Democratic television commercial. Common sense—if not empirical evidence—suggests that something likes this does occur. However, there is no factual basis for believing that most voters successfully avoid all political information that is in conflict with their present views. Most Americans are unavoidably exposed to political ideas and values with which they do not agree.

A clear example of a situation in which selective exposure almost certainly does not operate is the television debates between presidential candidates. Here it would be practically impossible to ignore one candidate and pay attention to the other. The debates illustrate the substantial impact of the mass media under the right circumstances. Nearly everyone in the American electorate watches one or more presidential television debates during a campaign. According to several different public opinion polls in 1960, about half of the voters reported that they were influenced by the debates in their evaluation of Kennedy and Nixon. Generalizing from survey results, it appears that several million voters based their choice of candidates solely on the debates. Among voters reporting that the debates determined their vote

---

[15]Patterson and McClure, *Political Advertising*, pp. 32–33.

choice, Kennedy held an advantage of three to one over Nixon.[16] It is not clear to what extent the presidential debates in 1976 influenced voters' choices between Ford and Carter, although more than 80 percent of the voters watched at least one of them. Based on the date of interviewing respondents in the 1976 CPS election study, Arthur Miller[17] reported that the amount of information that respondents had about the candidates and the perceived differences between candidates increased over the course of the debates. The informational role of the debates, if not their persuasive power, seems clear.

The Reagan-Mondale debates in 1984 appeared to have considerable potential for impact on vote choice. In the first debate the president appeared inept; commentators and the public quickly agreed he had "lost" the debate. Reagan's poor performance seems to have had absolutely no influence on the choice voters were making between him and Mondale. Perhaps if the second debate had turned out badly for President Reagan, some impact on vote choice would have materialized, but in that debate Reagan managed to hold his own and the last opportunity for Mondale to make large gains passed. The 1984 debates probably symbolized the hazards they pose to front-runners and the wisdom of Reagan's campaign managers to have him debate as seldom as possible.

In recent campaigns no other opportunity for winning over so many uncommitted voters or converting opponents has compared with the television debates. However, another significant political opportunity regularly offered candidates is the party nominating convention. A large television audience is available to each party during the convention, but holding the attention of the audience for extended periods of time appears to be difficult, particularly if there is no contest for the presidential nomination. Furthermore, strong partisans follow their party's convention more intently than other members of the electorate. The battle-marred Democratic convention in 1968 and McGovern's acceptance speech long after midnight in 1972 represent dramatic failures to use this opportunity to benefit the party's nominee.

Probably of greater import than the persuasive power of the mass media in a presidential contest is the media's ability to make potential

---

[16]Recomputed from Elihu Katz and Jacob J. Feldman, "The Debates in the Light of Research: A Survey of Surveys," *The Great Debates: Background, Perspective, Effects*, ed. Sidney Kraus (Bloomington: Indiana University Press, 1962), p. 212.

[17]*ISR Newsletter*, Vol. 6, No. 1, 1978, p. 5.

nominees well-known to the public or to consign them to obscurity. Patterson's study of the role of the media in 1976 shows that during the primaries, Carter benefited from the tendency of the press to cover only the winner of a primary, regardless of the narrowness of the victory or the number of convention delegates won. During the primary season, 50 percent of the press coverage of Democratic candidates went to Carter; Udall was second with about 15 percent. In the two cities studied, voter recognition of Carter rose from 20 percent to 80 percent in the same time period while Udall's increased from 23 to 36 percent.[18]

Even the accident of winning primaries in the Eastern time zone gave Carter disproportionately large coverage on evenings when other candidates enjoyed bigger victories further West.[19] It is important to realize that while the media doubtless contributed to the Carter bandwagon in 1976, this was possible because few voters were well informed about or committed to any of the many Democratic candidates. During the same period the media exaggerated the significance of Ford's early primary victories without noticeably influencing the public's feelings about him or Reagan.[20] It is much more difficult to influence voters with well-informed preferences.

Impact of Election Campaigns

Although most professional politicians take for granted the efficacy of political campaigns, scholarly analysis has often questioned their impact. In most elections the majority of voters decide how they will vote before the campaign begins. Beyond this, the general low level of political information in the American electorate throws doubt on the ability of undecided voters to absorb ideas during a campaign.

Perhaps two aspects of the problem should be distinguished in assessing the impact of political campaigns. The first is the overall impact on the total electorate, but the evidence indicates that the vote choice of most voters is not affected by political campaigns. The sec-

---

[18]Thomas E. Patterson, "Press Coverage and Candidate Success in Presidential Primaries: The 1976 Democratic Race," paper presented at the annual meeting of the American Political Science Association, Washington, D.C., 1977.

[19]James D. Barber (ed.), *Race for the Presidency* (Englewood Cliffs, N.J.: Prentice-Hall, 1978), chaps. 2–4.

[20]Patterson, *The Mass Media Election*, pp. 130–132.

ond is the possibility that campaigning influences a small but crucial proportion of the electorate, and many elections are close enough that the winning margin could be a result of the campaign. Clearly, professional politicians drive themselves and their organizations to influence every remaining undecided voter in the hope and expectation that they are providing or maintaining a winning margin.

One way of approaching the question of campaign impact is to see how many voters make up their minds before the campaign starts. Table 7–2 shows that in presidential elections from 1948 to 1984 voters made their vote choice at about the same time: in most years about one-third of the electorate decided before the conventions, another one-third decided during the conventions, and a final one-third decided during the campaign. The 1956 rematch between Stevenson and an extremely popular Eisenhower was the most deviant election, where well over half of the voters made a decision on how they would vote before the convention. In 1964 and 1972, with incumbents also running, more than 40 percent made up their minds before the conventions, and in 1984 half the voters did so. In contrast, voters, by a large margin, delayed their decisions longer in 1976 and 1980 than in earlier elections. Even with an incumbent in the race almost half of the voters did not make up their minds until sometime during the campaign. About 15 percent did not make a final choice until the last few days before the election.

The decision times of partisans and independents vary because the loyal party votes line up early behind the party's candidate. In all recent elections, the independents and weak partisans were more likely to make up their minds during the campaign, while strong partisans characteristically made their decisions by the end of the conventions. To put it differently, the less committed are still undecided at the start of the campaign. In fairly close elections, this relatively uncommitted group can still swing the election either way.

It is widely reported that the most interested voters make their vote decisions early and that the least interested voters remain undecided during the campaign. A great deal has been made of this generalization and its implications for campaign strategy. Essentially, the consideration has taken this form: the least interested (and least concerned and least informed) are the only voters still available during the campaign. And, in order to influence them, very simple campaign appeals are necessary. The interested voters (mainly partisan and already committed) are held in line with appeals to party loyalty.

This description is appropriate for some recent campaigns, but it is not a permanent characteristic of the American electorate. It fits the

TABLE 7-2 Distribution of Time of Decision on Vote Choice for President, 1948–1984

Time of Decision	1948	1952	1956	1960	1964	1968	1972	1976	1980	1984
Before conventions	37%	34%	57%	30%	40%	33%	43%	33%	42%	49%
During conventions	28	31	18	30	25	22	17	20	17	16
During campaign	25	31	21	36	33	38	35	45	40	29
Don't remember, not ascertained	10	4	4	4	3	7	4	2	1	5
Total	100%	100%	100%	100%	101%	100%	99%	100%	100%	99%
n =	424	1251	1285	1445	1126	1039	1119	1667	958	1376

Source: Survey Research Center/Center for Political Studies National Election Studies.

Eisenhower elections and perhaps the later Roosevelt elections as well as the elections beginning in 1976. Interest was not particularly high in the 1984 campaign but the most interested voters made their decisions before the nominating conventions. Those voters who remained undecided into the last two months before election day revealed very little interest in the campaign. In contrast, in 1960, the least interested voters showed a slight tendency to decide early rather than late; in 1964, 1968, and 1972, the time of decision of the most interested and least interested was no different. In other words, under many circumstances interested voters are as likely as uninterested voters to enter the campaign still undecided on their vote choice. This is not to say that these interested voters are completely without preferences or that they are extremely well informed. They are neither. But it is not true that in all political campaigns the only voters still undecided at the start of the campaign are uninterested in politics.

Campaign Strategy

Material from this and the previous chapter can be used as a basis for generalizing about political communication and campaign effects from the perspective of a candidate. In political campaigns, candidates stand little chance of altering the electorate's issue preferences on policies that are sufficiently salient to affect their vote choices. In the short run, to change individuals' preferences on issues that they care about is difficult by any means, and it is particularly difficult through the impersonal content of mass media. To change an individual's preferences or pattern of behavior, personal contact is more effective than the media; so vote choice or turnout are likely to be influenced, if at all, by an acquaintance of the individual.

To a limited degree, candidates can alter the salience of a few issues for some segments of the public, but their capacity to increase or decrease the importance of issues is slight in comparison with what will happen in the ordinary course of events. For example, a candidate cannot make corruption in government a salient issue solely through his or her campaign, but a major scandal can make it an issue whether the candidates want it or not. Nevertheless, it is worth some effort to increase the salience of issues that are expected to benefit the candidate, even though that effort will probably fail. Correspondingly, to attempt to reduce the salience of issues that hurt a candidate is worth some effort, although, again, this strategy is not likely to succeed.

Much more susceptible to change are the public's perceptions of candidates' positions on issues. News and advertising through the mass media can convey a lot of information on issue stands and dramatize the differences between candidates. The more factual this information and the more the candidates agree on the respective characterizations, the more fully this information is absorbed by the public. This is the area of attitude change and public awareness in which candidates can accomplish the most.

In the final analysis, candidates are most interested in winning votes, regardless of how strong a preference each vote represents; but there are grounds for wanting large numbers of supporters with very strong preferences. Individuals with an overwhelming preference, holding no significant conflicting views, form the base of support for a candidate that yields campaign contributions and workers. These are the individuals all through society who casually influence the people around them to hold views favorable to a candidate. These are the opinion leaders who interpret and misinterpret the news on behalf of their candidate.

The more obviously partisan or one-sided the content of either media message or personal contact, the less likely it is to influence the uncommitted, not to mention the hostile. This poses a problem for the campaigner. Even though extreme messages are most likely to attract the attention of the relatively apathetic uncommitted voter, those same messages are least likely to get results. For this reason, in part, events dramatizing an issue can be so valuable or damaging to a candidate. Events that affect a candidate's personal image are especially important because these perceptions are the most difficult to change through direct appeals in campaign advertising.

The overall implications of this discussion are several. It takes a long time and probably noncampaign periods of low intensity to switch individual issue stands or party loyalties. The media presentation and personal discussion of political and social conditions or events have a greater impact on attitudes than advertising or party contacts.

To a considerable degree, these generalizations about political influence and communication imply that by the time a candidate wins nomination, he or she faces a constituency whose basic values and preferences can be changed only by events over which the candidate probably has little or no control. The only impact the candidate can have through campaigning is to make issue positions known as dramatically as possible and to contrast those positions with the opponent's. No candidate will know in advance what the net effect of these efforts will be, and most will never know. But most elections are contested under conditions that give one candidate a great initial advantage in the partisan loyalty and issue preferences of the constituency. The best chance for candidates is to exploit what they believe are their advantages, but in most cases the stable party loyalties and unchanging issue preferences of a constituency impose significant constraints on how much difference campaign strategies can make.

8

Political Culture and Socialization

☆☆☆

In the preceding chapters we have noted some significant trends over the last two decades, most notably a decline in voting turnout and a decline in partisanship. The first of these, in particular, has been linked to other, more fundamental attitudes toward the political system—a decline in trust in governmental institutions and a decline in citizens' beliefs in their ability to influence governmental decisions. In this chapter we will turn to a consideration of these and other basic orientations toward the American political system. The main focus will be on a broad pattern of beliefs that form part of the political culture and, secondarily, on the acquisition of these beliefs. A distinction also will be made, where appropriate, between the beliefs of political leaders and of the mass public, since a basic finding is that their beliefs about the political system are quite dissimilar. The discussion of political culture will cover attitudes toward the goals and procedures of a democracy, attitudes toward the role of individual participants in the system, and the implications of these attitudes for political action. Finally, the content of American political culture will be examined as a foundation for democracy.

Attention will of necessity focus on the values of the dominant national culture. Of course, socialization processes exist in political subcultures that may promote contrary values and attitudes. The United States offers an extremely complex political culture for analysis, and it may be unfortunate that so difficult an analytic task has been the main focus of investigations in socialization and political culture. Without being cynical, one can still be discouraged over the findings in this area of research. A number of major studies during the past two decades have contributed to great interest in socialization and political culture but have been less successful in creating a structure of theoretically significant relationships.

Democratic Beliefs and Values

A major thrust of the analysis of democratic political systems and the United States in particular has been the search for a fundamental, underlying set of widely supported values. Presumably, the commitment to these principles holds a democratic society together in the presence of conflict and provides support and legitimacy for the functioning of its political institutions.

A distinction often is made between democratic goals—such as equality, individual freedom, and due process of law—and democratic procedures—such as majority rule and protection of the political rights of freedom of speech, press, and assembly. The distinction is an important one to make when the extent to which these ideals are supported in the political culture of a system is under consideration, for democratic goals can quite possibly be pursued through undemocratic means or democratic procedures can be used for antidemocratic ends. Likewise, mass support may exist for democratic goals but not for democratic procedures, or vice versa.

A widely held and perfectly plausible expectation is that the American public supports both of these kinds of democratic values. At a highly abstract level this is true enough. American citizens overwhelmingly subscribe to the basic rules and goals of democracy when this commitment is kept vague and abstract. As individuals are asked about more and more precise applications of democratic principles, agreement disappears. Specifically, the American electorate cannot seem to reach widespread agreement on extending civil rights and liberties to individuals with unpopular political and social opinions or agreement on extending social and economic equality to certain ethnic and racial minorities. For example, a 1971 survey by the National

Opinion Research Center[1] found 95 percent willing to support the right of a group of their neighbors to circulate a petition, but only 52 percent willing to support a similar right for a group wishing to legalize the use of marijuana.

During recent decades there has been an increased willingness in the public to allow free speech on unpopular points of view and permit books with distasteful perspectives to remain in libraries. Numerous studies document this shift in attitudes from the mid-1950s to the 1970s and without exception they find a strong relationship between tolerance and education.[2]

Two important qualifications are in order. First, the electorate's responses are attitudes that may have little meaning for them and are not measures of their behavior or even measures of their attitudes under crisis or threat to democratic principles.

The second important qualification of these findings applies to the political, social, and economic leaders in American society who consistently support these democratic principles more strongly than the general public does. Support among leaders is usually so high that it is possible to conclude that the leaders in society defend and maintain democratic procedures. The leaders' consensus on democratic rights and values makes the weakness of the general public less crucial. National studies by Stouffer and McClosky support the view that leaders are stronger than the public in support of "rules of the game."[3] Table 8-1 from McClosky's study shows the degree to which leaders support the "rules of the game" in comparison with the public. Political influentials—in this study delegates and alternates to the Democratic and Republican national conventions in 1956—are consistently more likely to agree with "rules of the game" than is a sample of the electorate. It may not be reassuring to discover that 6.8 percent of the

---

[1]Cited in Kenneth Prewitt and Sidney Verba, *An Introduction to American Government* (New York: Harper & Row, 1974), pp. 87–88.

[2]For the major study of the 1950s, see Samuel Stouffer, *Communism, Conformity and Civil Liberties* (Garden City, N.Y.: Doubleday, 1955); for more recent work, see C. Z. Nunn, H. J. Crockett, and J. A. Williams, *Tolerance for Nonconformity* (San Francisco: Jossey-Ross, 1978); James Piereson, John L. Sullivan, and George Marcus, "Political Tolerance: An Overview and Some New Findings," *The Electorate Reconsidered*, ed. John C. Pierce and John L. Sullivan (Beverly Hills, Calif.: Sage Publications, 1980), pp. 157–178.

[3]Samuel Stouffer, *Communism, Conformity and Civil Liberties*; Herbert McClosky, "Consensus and Ideology in American Politics," *American Political Science Review* 58 (June 1964): 361–382.

political influentials agreed that "the majority has the right to abolish minorities if it wants to" or that 13.3 percent agreed that "almost any unfairness or brutality may have to be justified when some great purpose is being carried out." But in both examples substantially greater proportions, one-quarter and one-third respectively, of the general electorate supported these views.

TABLE 8–1 Political Influentials vs. the Electorate: Response to Items Expressing Belief in Democratic Values[a]

Items	Percent Agreeing with Item: Political Influentials	General Electorate
There are times when it almost seems better for the people to take the law into their own hands rather than wait for the machinery of government to act.	13.3%	26.9%
The majority has the right to abolish minorities if it wants to.	6.8%	28.4%
If congressional committees stuck strictly to the rules and gave every witness his rights, they would never succeed in exposing the many dangerous subversives they have turned up.	24.7%	47.4%
I don't mind a politician's methods if he manages to get the right things done.	25.6%	42.4%
Almost any unfairness or brutality may have to be justified when some great purpose is being carried out.	13.3%	32.8%
People ought to be allowed to vote even if they can't do so intelligently.	65.5%	47.6%
The true American way of life is disappearing so fast that we may have to use force to save it.	12.8%	34.6%
n =	3020	1484

[a]Since respondents were forced to make a choice on each item, the number of omitted or "don't know" responses was, on the average, fewer than 1 percent and thus has little influence on the direction or magnitude of the results reported in this table.

Source: Herbert McClosky, "Consensus and Ideology in American Politics," *American Political Science Review* 58 (1964): Table 1, p. 365.

More recently Jeane Kirkpatrick[4] studied the attitudes of political leaders, focusing on delegates to the 1972 Democratic and Republican national conventions. Although the study is more concerned with issues than principles, her findings suggest the earlier pattern still exists. For example, among leaders, 17 percent endorse abridging the rights of the accused in order to stop criminal activity, while in the public as a whole 46 percent support stopping crime even at the risk of reducing rights.[5]

Presumably, leaders are recruited and educated in such a way that they come prepared with, or develop, agreement on democratic procedures. Apparently leaders make decisions that maintain democratic practices, even without widespread public support. A somewhat less comforting possibility is that the political elite is simply sophisticated enough to understand what is the "correct" answer to attitude questions dealing with democratic beliefs. The seemingly greater adherence to these values by the politically active would attest to the prominence of such norms in the mass political culture but would not necessarily suggest any great commitment to nor willingness to abide by these values. Some of the least palatable aspects of Watergate suggest no great depth of appreciation of these principles on the part of some prominent members of the Nixon administration, and later revelations suggest the same about earlier liberal administrations like that of Kennedy.

The widespread interest by political analysts in public opinion and democratic beliefs has been based partly on a somewhat mistaken impression. Stable democratic political systems have been assumed to rest on a nearly universal commitment to fundamental principles and their application, but the evidence on this point is inconclusive. Certainly, a democratic system cannot long survive widespread, intense hostility to democratic values, but probably positive belief in particular operating procedures among the public is unnecessary. Hostility to democratic procedures is fatal, whether among the leaders or the public, but support of these procedures may prove essential only among leaders. Perhaps the public need not agree on basic principles so long as it does not demand disruptive policies and procedures.

---

[4]Jeane Kirkpatrick, *The New Presidential Elite* (New York: Russell Sage Foundation and the Twentieth Century Fund, 1976).

[5]These data are recomputed from Kirkpatrick, *The New Presidential Elite*, Table 10.3, p. 302.

Childhood Socialization

Most social groups, particularly those with distinctive sets of norms and values, make some effort to teach these attitudes and expected behaviors to their new members. In most societies, this process of socialization is focused primarily on the largest group of new members, children. It is through the process of political socialization that the political culture of a society is transmitted from one generation to the next, but this socialization is also an important mechanism through which change in the political culture can take place. In societies in which most learning about politics takes place in the home, the prevailing political culture probably changes no faster than the attitudes of the adult population as a whole, in response to varied personal experiences and changing circumstances in the environment. In modern societies other agents of political socialization also are involved, particularly the educational system and, increasingly, the mass media. To the extent that these institutions instill a different set of values and norms in comparison with those held by the adult population as a whole, there is an opportunity for changing the political culture. In the Soviet Union and the People's Republic of China, where the official ideology has completely dominated both the schools and the mass communications system, massive changes in values have taken place within the span of a generation. In the United States, more diversity in views is permitted, but the prevalence of middle-class values among both teachers and the media guarantees that these orientations will continue to be widespread in the population as a whole.

Given the importance of the socialization process in the transmission of the fundamental beliefs and values of the political culture, it is surprising that the many recent socialization studies have not paid much attention to the development of attitudes supportive of democratic goals and procedures. Data collected by Easton and Hess[6] show that children develop an affective attachment to the term *democracy* very early (about the third grade), but the concept acquires meaning much more slowly. Figure 8–1 shows the progress of this learning for several perceptions from the fourth grade to the eighth grade; however, perhaps the most interesting aspect of this figure is the high level of

---

[6]The results of this study have been reported in several articles and in Robert D. Hess and Judith V. Torney, *The Development of Political Attitudes in Children* (Chicago: Aldine, 1967); and David Easton and Jack Dennis, *Children in the Political System: Origins of Political Legitimacy* (New York: McGraw-Hill, 1969).

FIGURE 8-1 Children's Understanding of the Concept of Democracy According to Grade Level

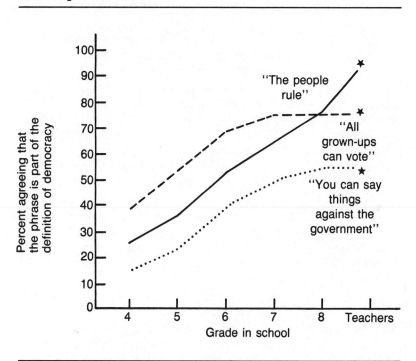

Source: Robert D. Hess and Judith V. Torney, *The Development of Political Attitudes in Children* (New York: Anchor Books, 1968), Table 13, p. 75.

disagreement among teachers over the correctness of including the right of dissent in the meaning of democracy. Other studies have shown that adolescents are somewhat more likely to endorse democratic values than their parents, but the process through which these ideals are learned, and the extent to which children learn to apply them to concrete situations, remain to be studied.

More emphasis has been placed on the development of the child's thinking about the institutions of government and about his or her own role as a citizen. The child's first view of government and governmental leaders casts them as all-powerful but benevolent, undoubtedly the result of the twin objectives of parents and teachers to instill an acceptance of authority and to shield young children from the harsher realities of political life. Gradually, the child acquires a more realistic and more cynical view of the world. Children also begin with a very personalized view of government; government means the president or, for some, the police officer. In time, these images are replaced or supplemented with more abstract ideas about Congress and the election process.[7]

Throughout the socialization process, there are important differences in development associated with social class and intelligence as measured by IQ tests. Generally, this takes the form of learning and adopting the teacher's values more quickly, often with rather intriguing results. Adopting a partisan stance would be considered taboo in most American classrooms, but advocating nonpartisanship is not. An overwhelming majority of the teachers in the Easton and Hess sample thought it preferable to "vote for the person" rather than join a political party. Children progressively adopt this view as they move through the elementary grades, and middle-class and high-IQ children do so at higher rates than others.[8] Some 87 percent of the teachers saw the United Nations as more influential than the United States in keeping world peace and, by a two-to-one margin, teachers believe Congress has more to do with "running the country" than the president. Children learn these perceptions, inaccuracies and all, with the better students absorbing them faster.

During the elementary grades, children also develop a set of attitudes toward their own role as citizens. Initially, the emphasis is on obedience: the good citizen obeys the law, just as good children obey their parents. In the American socialization process, this is gradually replaced by a view of oneself as a more active participant in the political system. The good citizen is one who votes, and still later, the child adds to this the notion that government can be influenced through the voting process. The data from *The Civic Culture* by Almond and Verba[9] suggest that the socialization process in the United States instills this set of attitudes in its citizens more successfully than some other western democracies. Americans are more likely to view themselves as "participants" as opposed to "subjects" than are citizens of the United Kingdom, Germany, Italy, or Mexico. In all the countries studied, experiences with democratic decision making, in the schools or in the family, were related to adult participation in politics and to

---

[7]David Easton and Jack Dennis, "The Child's Image of Government," *Socialization to Politics: A Reader*, ed. Jack Dennis (New York: John Wiley & Sons, 1973), p. 67.

[8]Hess and Torney, *The Development of Political Attitudes in Children*.

[9]Gabriel Almond and Sidney Verba, *The Civic Culture* (Princeton, N.J.: Princeton University Press, 1963).

the belief that the individual can influence government. Other studies have documented that, within the United States, children's attitudes toward their own possible effectiveness vis-à-vis government are related to social class and that social class, in turn, is related to differences in the attitude toward authority within the home. Working-class parents are more likely to demand obedience and allow less input from children in the familial decision-making process than are middle-class parents. As a result, their children are less likely to see themselves as able to influence authority or to participate successfully in politics.

As with other attitudes, development of confidence in one's own ability to influence government is related to social class and intelligence among children, just as it is related to social class and education in adults. Some other aspects of the view of the citizen's role that children develop in the later elementary years might conceivably hinder their effectiveness or willingness to participate in the real world of politics later on. The role of the individual in influencing government is stressed; the role of organized group activity in politics is downgraded. Similarly, children in the American culture develop a low tolerance for conflict, believing, for example, that it hurts the country when the political parties disagree.

Citizen Roles and System Support

American citizens have a strongly developed sense of obligation to inform themselves, to participate in elections, and, to a lesser extent, to participate in other forms of political activity. About 90 percent of all adults believe it is the duty of good citizens to vote in elections, although obviously many of them do not act on that commitment at every election. Although Americans also believe in the importance of informing themselves about political and governmental affairs, they readily concede that in most cases they personally are not as well informed as they should be.

The expectations an individual develops about how the political process functions often are not satisfied in reality. When clear expectations are not met in the behavior of political leaders or in the experiences individuals have in the political process, disappointment, cynicism, or hostility may result. Americans come to hold rather high expectations for the political system and, consequently, are subject to considerable disenchantment with the performance of government and their own role in politics. Although no direct evidence on this point is available, nothing has been found to suggest that the value Americans place on the ideals of democracy, majority rule, or the importance of participation in politics has declined. Rather, events over the last two decades led to a larger perceived discrepancy between the specific American political institutions (and their incumbents) and the ideal. The result was a twenty-year decline in the levels of trust and confidence in the institutions of American government, beginning in the late 1950s and continuing throughout the 1960s and 1970s. One of the noteworthy accomplishments—or at least accompaniments—of the Reagan presidency has been to halt and reverse this trend.

Figure 8–2 documents the steady decline in trust in government from 1958 to 1980. The only exception during this period is the increase in positive attitudes among blacks in 1964, occasioned by the early successes of the civil rights movement. The long-term decline in trust and confidence in government was accelerated by the Watergate-related disclosures. These changes involved some of the most

FIGURE 8–2 Trust in Government According to Race, 1958–1984

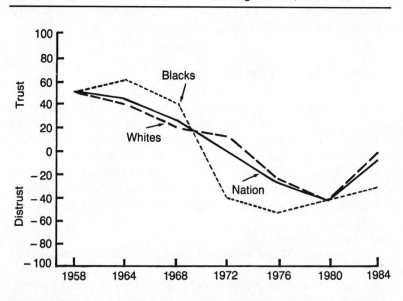

Source: Arthur H. Miller, Thad A. Brown, and Alden S. Raine, "Social Conflict and Political Estrangement, 1958–1972," paper presented at the Midwest Political Science Association meeting, Chicago, 1973, Figure 2; Center for Political Studies National Election Studies.

basic evaluations of the political system: increasing proportions of the population believed that "public officials don't care much what people like me think" and expressed lack of confidence that the institutions of government will do the right thing. Interestingly, the problems of President Nixon and the resulting confrontation with Congress and the courts hurt the esteem in which the presidency was held without doing much to improve the image of Congress or the Supreme Court.

Even though the Watergate scandals and related matters had a disastrous impact on Nixon's popularity, the general decline in respect for and trust in governmental institutions like the presidency began some time before. Curiously, this pattern of declining prestige extended to many nongovernmental institutions, such as the news media, schools, and the professions. Furthermore, the trend exists outside the United States in many of the developed nations of the world. Whatever the consequences of this trend, the causes are not limited to a few sensational political scandals.

The very low levels of trust shown in Figure 8-2 for both whites and blacks through 1980 represent further declines from the post-Watergate levels of trust in 1974.[10] In this respect the Ford administration did not accomplish one of its avowed purposes of restoring trust and confidence in government. President Carter made an even more widely publicized attempt to renew the public's trust in him. When public opinion polls showed that he was suffering the same gradual decline in approval that other presidents had known, Carter responded by declaring the country in the grip of a social malaise and asking the public to have more confidence in him. This appeal had no discernible impact on trust in the president.

The years of the Reagan presidency have witnessed a noticeable increase in trust, virtually all attributable to the changing attitudes of whites. This substantial upturn in trust appears related to the upbeat mood created by the Reagan administration and to a mild restoration of confidence in many public and private institutions in American society. Nevertheless, the public's trust in government is currently at about the same level as it was following Watergate. The continuation of this upward trend and its permanency remain to be seen.

---

[10]For a discussion of the factors that caused the decline in trust, see Arthur H. Miller, "Political Issues and Trust in Government: 1964–1970," and Jack Citrin, "Comment," *The American Political Science Review* 68 (September 1974): 951–988.

In the past, the youngest voters were typically the most trusting of government, a tendency one would expect, given their recent exposure to the educational process that tries to build support for the system. As late as the early 1960s, when most of the major socialization studies reported to date were undertaken, young people entered adulthood with strong affective feeling toward the government and a positive orientation toward themselves as participants in it.

A study of high school seniors and their parents, carried out in 1965 by M. Kent Jennings,[11] showed that trust and confidence in government were fairly high among the students. Learning, of course, continues into adulthood, and substantial modification of attitudes can occur through a variety of personal experiences with politics, new group memberships, and the like.

If a group shares experiences, their attitudes may be affected in a distinctive way. For example, attitudes of political support among adult black Americans increased temporarily in the early 1960s, concomitant with the growth of the civil rights movement (see Figure 8–2). The turbulent end of the 1960s had the opposite effect on the levels of trust among young people. In 1973, re-interviews of the students in the Jennings study showed that their level of trust had declined markedly and was accompanied by an increase in cynicism.[12] These changes were considerably greater than the changes in their parents' attitudes over the eight years, although the young people were still somewhat more supportive than their parents. The 1972 Center for Political Studies survey showed that the young people in the sample were the least trusting of government of any age group, a stark reversal of findings in earlier years when young people were generally the most trusting. It is possible that when dramatic changes occur, they are felt most intensely among those groups with the least firmly established attitudes. By the mid-1970s, the earlier pattern had returned and once again young people were more trusting than older people.

These general attitudes of distrust of and dissatisfaction with the government have a parallel in the declining confidence of individuals

---

[11]The findings of this study are most extensively reported in M. Kent Jennings and Richard G. Niemi, *The Political Character of Adolescence: The Influence of Families and Schools* (Princeton, N.J.: Princeton University Press, 1974), and *Generation and Politics* (Princeton, N.J.: Princeton University Press, 1981).

[12]These observations are based on data provided with Paul A. Beck, Jere W. Bruner, and L. Douglas Dobson, *Political Socialization: Inheritance and Durability of Parental Political Views* (Washington, D.C.: ASPA/ICPSR, 1974).

TABLE 8-2 Political Efficacy, 1952–1984

Responses to the statement, "People like me don't have any say about what government does"	1952	1956	1960	1964	1968	1972	1976	1980	1984
Agree	31%	28%	27%	29%	41%	40%	41%	39%	33%
Disagree	68	71	72	70	58	59	56	59	66
Don't know, not ascertained	1	1	1	1	1	1	3	2	1
Total	100%	100%	100%	100%	100%	100%	100%	100%	100%
n =	1799	1762	1954	1571	1337	2705	2403	1408	1978

Source: Survey Research Center/Center for Political Studies National Election Studies.

183

in their ability to participate effectively in the political process. Table 8-2 shows a long trend in the individual's sense of political efficacy, that is, in the individual's belief about his or her ability to influence government. Between 1964 and 1968, about 10 percent of the public shifted to feeling they had little influence. Like trust in government, attitudes of political efficacy turned upward during the Reagan years. By 1984, political efficacy had returned to about the same level as in 1952. This pattern is not nearly as dramatic as the changes in trust in government, which indicate that individuals had not lost as much confidence in themselves as they had in their leaders. There always are differences among individuals in their sense of political efficacy, differences that are strongly related to education, general self-confidence, and experience with political participation. However, the decline in the overall level of feelings of efficacy at the same time that general levels of education were being raised suggests that the decline is attributable to changes in the political environment, rather than to any changes in individual characteristics, such as skills or general self-confidence.

Protest and Violence

In recent years protests and demonstrations have become common mechanisms for voicing political opinions and pursuing political goals. In a time when rather staid and conservative groups adopt such tactics, it is well to remember that twenty years ago, protests were seen as disruptive and their legitimacy in a democratic system was open to question. Their use and acceptance increased throughout the years of the Civil Rights and anti-war movements of the 1960s. Even groups that condemned these particular causes saw their usefulness as television, with its need for action footage for news coverage, gave nationwide exposure to protest marchers and demonstrators.

Table 8-3 shows the change in attitudes toward both peaceful demonstrations and violent protests between 1968 and 1972, the period of most intense anti-war activity. Most Americans did not approve of either peaceful or violent protests, with less than one in ten approving of violent, disruptive activities. Over this time period, however, the level of opposition to such activities declined, with increasing numbers of Americans apparently willing to tolerate demonstrations and protests under some circumstances.

If these relationships persist into the future, increasingly greater tolerance, but not necessarily more widespread participation, can be

TABLE 8-3 Attitudes Toward Peaceful Demonstrations and Disruptive Protests, 1968 and 1972

Attitudes toward:	1968	1972
Peaceful Demonstrations		
Approve	18%	18%
Pro-Con, it depends	25	40
Disapprove	49	40
Don't know, not ascertained	8	2
Total	100%	100%
Disruptive Protests		
Approve	7%	8%
Pro-Con, it depends	16	33
Disapprove	67	57
Don't know, not ascertained	10	3
Total	100%	101%
n =	1344	2705

Source: Survey Research Center/Center for Political Studies National Election Studies.

anticipated. As Table 8–4 shows, the younger members of the electorate are more likely to approve of peaceful demonstrations than are older citizens, and among those under age thirty, more approve than disapprove of peaceful demonstrations. Perhaps as these individuals grow older, their attitudes will become more disapproving, but it is as likely that the public will gradually shift toward more tolerance of protest. In data not shown, there is also a relationship between education and approval of peaceful demonstrations that is independent of the age relationship. Among college graduates under age thirty, more than 50 percent approve of peaceful demonstrations, and only about 10 percent disapprove.

These relationships suggest that as education levels increase, approval of demonstrations will increase. Nevertheless, it is not clear whether these attitudes reflect greater tolerance toward the deviant behavior of others or more hostility toward the political system. We are inclined to believe that these attitudes do not testify to hostile, anti-system feelings on the part of younger, better educated Americans but rather indicate a willingness to accept demonstrations as part of political life. Beyond this, these attitudes suggest a growing unwillingness to be repressive against political interests expressed through peaceful demonstrations, perhaps because the claims of participants

TABLE 8-4 Attitudes Toward Peaceful Demonstrations According to Age, 1972

Attitudes	Age			
	18-29	*30-45*	*46-64*	*65 and over*
Approve	29%	20%	13%	9%
Pro-Con, it depends	50	42	37	25
Disapprove	20	38	48	61
Don't know, not ascertained	1	1	2	4
Total	100%	101%	100%	99%
n =	744	722	790	432

Source: Center for Political Studies 1972 National Election Study.

are granted some legitimacy. Disruptive violence is less acceptable to the public, though the same relationships with age and education exist at a lower level.

In their analysis of young people between 1965 and 1973, Jennings and Niemi were able to show that college students who engaged in protest activities were more interested in and informed about politics than nonprotestors. There are differences between the two groups in their political feelings and evaluations, but the protestors could not be characterized as alienated or anti-system.[13] Peaceful demonstrations or strikes—activities engaged in by millions of Americans—do not seem to disrupt the individual's orientation to politics.

Certainly, one of the more important aspects of political culture is its relevance to the maintenance of the political system. Belief in democratic ideals is viewed as essential to the preservation of a democratic system, both because such beliefs inhibit citizens from undemocratic actions and because the public will demand proper behavior on the part of political leaders.

In these terms, there is some uneasiness about the public support for American democracy—and perhaps for any democratic regime. It is possible to view the United States as a democratic system that has survived without a strong democratic political culture because governmental policies have gained continual, widespread acceptance. If

---

[13]Jennings and Niemi, *Generation and Politics*, chap. 11.

that satisfaction erodes, however, the public has no deep commitment to democratic values and processes that will inhibit support of anti-democratic leaders or disruptive activities.

Democratic theory implies that the public should demand values and procedures embodying democratic principles. There is the hope or expectation that the public in a democratic society will insist on certain values and processes. More precisely, it is argued that in the absence of insistence on particular values and procedures, democratic regimes will fail. Clearly, a mass public demanding democratic values and procedures is stronger support for a democratic system than a mass public merely willing to tolerate a democratic regime. This does not mean, however, that the stronger form of support is necessary for a democratic system, although superficially it appears desirable. Quite possibly, strong support is nearly impossible to attain, and weaker support is adequate, given other conditions.

In our view, the analysis of support for democratic regimes has been misguided by an emphasis on factors contributing to the establishment of democracy, not its maintenance. Stronger public support probably is required for the successful launching of a democracy than it is for maintaining an already established democracy. Possibly, preserving a regime simply requires that no substantial proportion of the society be actively hostile to the regime and engage in disruptive activities. In other words, absence of disruptive acts, not the presence of supportive attitudes, is crucial.

On the other hand, the positive support by leaders for a political system is essential to its existence. If some leaders are willing to oppose the system, it is crucial that there be no substantial number of followers to which the leaders can appeal. The followers' attitudes, as opposed to their willingness to act themselves, may provide a base of support for anti-system behavior by leaders. In this sense, unanimous public support for democratic principles would be a more firm basis for a democratic system.

The increasing levels of dissatisfaction, accompanied by a lack of strong commitment to democratic values in the American public, appear to create some potential for public support of undemocratic leaders. In this light, the public's loyalty to political parties and commitment to traditional processes that inhibit aspiring undemocratic leaders become all the more important.

APPENDIX A

Survey Research Methods

—————————— ☆☆☆ ——————————

Many of the data in this book have come from survey research, and most of the analysis reported has been based on findings from survey research. For more than two decades, the data from the national election studies of the Survey Research Center and the Center for Political Studies, as well as from other major survey projects in political science, have been available through the Inter-university Consortium for Political and Social Research and have formed the basis for countless research projects in many fields by scholars, graduate students, and undergraduates. Given this widespread use of survey data, it is appropriate to give some description of the data collection methods that underlie them.

During the last forty years, social scientists have developed an impressive array of techniques for discovering and measuring individual attitudes and behavior. Basically, survey research relies on giving a standard questionnaire to the individuals to be studied. And in most major studies of the national electorate, trained interviewers ask the questions and record the responses in a face-to-face interview with each respondent. A few studies depend on the respondents themselves filling out the questionnaires. Recently, the rising costs of survey research, the pressure for quick results, and the availability of random digit-dialing have led commercial pollsters to rely increasingly on telephone interviewing.

There are four data-collection phases of survey research: (1) sampling, (2) questionnaire constructing, (3) interviewing, and (4) coding. At most points the methods of the Survey Research Center at the University of Michigan will be described.

Sampling

It may seem inappropriate to analyze the entire American electorate using studies composed of fewer than two thousand individuals, which is about the average number of respondents in the studies used in this book. But it would be prohibitively expensive to interview the entire electorate, and the only way to study public opinion nationally is by interviewing relatively few individuals who accurately represent the entire electorate. Probability sampling is the method used to assure that the individuals selected for interviewing will be representative of the total population.

Probability sampling attempts to select respondents in such a way that every individual in the population has an equal chance of being selected for interviewing. If the respondents are selected in this way, the analyst can be confident that the characteristics of the sample are approximately the same as those of the whole population. It would be impossible to make a list of every adult in the United States and then draw names from the list randomly, so the Survey Research Center departs from such strict random procedures in three basic ways: the sample is *stratified, clustered,* and *of households.*

Stratification means that random selection occurs within subpopulations; in the United States the sample is customarily selected within regions to guarantee that all sections are represented and within communities of different sizes as well. *Clustering* means that relatively small geographical areas, called "primary sampling units," are randomly selected within the stratified categories so that many interviews are concentrated within a small area in order to reduce the costs and inconvenience for interviewers. Finally, the Survey Research Center samples *households* rather than individuals (although within households individuals are sampled and interviewed); this means that within sampling areas households are enumerated and selected at random. (This sampling procedure means that no respondents are selected on military bases, in hospitals, hotels, and prisons, or in other places where people do not live in households. However, after the enfranchisement of eighteen-year-olds the Survey Research Center began to include college dormitories as residences to be sampled.)

An alternative procedure for selecting respondents is quota sampling. The area where interviews are to be made may be picked by stratified sampling procedures, but at the last stage of selection the interviewer is given discretion to choose respondents according to quotas. Quotas usually cover several social characteristics, but the intention is to create a collection of respondents with proportions of quota-controlled characteristics identical to those in the population. For example, the quota might call for half the respondents to be men, half to be women; for one-third to be grade-school educated, one-third high-school educated, and one-third college educated; and so forth. The advantage of this procedure is that it is much faster and less expensive than probability sampling, but the disadvantages are severe. With quota sampling, the analyst cannot have confidence that respondents are representative of the total population because the interviewers introduce conscious or unconscious biases when selecting respondents. In the past, commercial polling organizations used quota sampling, which allowed the interviewer to have discretion over whom to interview. As a result, easily contacted people like retired persons or young women at home with small children, were likely to be overrepresented in the sample. Both methods of sampling depend heavily on the ability and integrity of the interviewers, but probability sampling does not permit interviewers to introduce biases. Most statistical techniques assume that probability sampling has been used in collecting the data.

Increasingly, the commercial polling organizations have turned to telephone interviewing as a faster and cheaper alternative to field interviewing. In 1984 pre-election polling, NBC, CBS/New York Times, and ABC/Washington Post all used similar sampling procedures for their telephone interviewing. Random digit-dialing is typically used by these polling operations to select both listed and unlisted numbers and to give each number the same chance of being called. Obviously this practice ignores individuals without telephones, but there are no major obstacles to drawing an excellent sample of telephone numbers. The problems begin at that point. Success in finding someone at home and completing a telephone interview is uneven and failures may run as high as 50 percent. Some polling organizations make repeated callbacks, and of course the chances of getting an answer increase with the number of callbacks.

Once the phone is answered, it is necessary to select a respondent from the household. Some randomizing procedure is typically used to select the respondent. If the respondent selected is not at home, either an appointment is arranged for a callback or the household is dropped. The more often respondents are lost in this way or refuse to be interviewed, the more the sample departs from its original design. These procedures are likely to generate a sample that is biased toward women so all the polling organizations usually take steps to counter this tendency. These organizations differ in the degree to which they weight the results to compensate for other demographical biases.[1]

Probability sampling can result in unrepresentative samples also. Of particular concern is the "nonresponse rate," that is, the number of respondents originally selected who refuse to be interviewed and thus do not appear in the sample. Should these nonrespondents share some characteristic disproportionately, the resulting sample will underrepresent that type of person. For example, if residents of high crime neighborhoods, or the elderly or alienated people refuse to be interviewed at higher rates than others, the sample will have fewer of these people than occur in the population and thus the sample will be biased. Currently, survey organizations have the greatest difficulty getting interviews in the inner cities of the largest metropolitan areas. The likelihood is high that the people who consent to be interviewed in these areas are different from, and not representative of, those who refuse.

Questionnaire Constructing

In survey questionnaires, several types of questions will ordinarily be used. Public opinion surveys began years ago with "forced-choice" questions that a respondent was asked to answer by choosing among a set of offered alternatives. For example, forced-choice questions frequently take the form of stating a position on public policy and asking the respondent to "agree" or "disagree" with the statement. The analysis in Chapter 5 was based in part on the answers to forced-choice questions on public policy that were used in Survey Research Center and Center for Political Studies questionnaires in which respondents were asked to "agree strongly," "agree," "disagree," or "disagree strongly." Some respondents either gave qualified answers that did not fit into these prearranged categories or had no opinions.

A major innovation associated with the Survey Research Center is the use of "open-ended questioning." Open-ended questions give re-

---

[1] *Public Opinion*, Vol. 4, No. 1 (Feb/Mar. 1981): 20.

spondents the opportunity to express their opinions in their own way without being forced to select among categories provided by the questionnaire. Questions like "Is there anything in particular you like about the Democratic party?" or "What are the most important problems facing the country today?" permit the respondents to answer in their own terms. Survey Research Center interviewers encourage respondents to answer such questions as fully as they can with neutral "probes" like "Could you tell me more about that?" "Anything else?" and similar queries that draw forth more discussion. There is no doubt that open-ended questions are a superior method of eliciting accurate expressions of opinion.

There are two major disadvantages to open-ended questioning: (1) it places much more of a burden on interviewers to record the responses; and (2) the burden of reducing the many responses to a dimension that can be analyzed is left for the coders. For example, if Americans are asked, "Do you think of yourself as a Democrat, a Republican, or an independent?" almost all of the responses will fit usefully into the designated categories:

1. Democrat
2. Independent
3. Republican
4. Other party
5. I'm nothing; apolitical
6. Don't know
7. Refused to say
8. Not ascertained

On the other hand, if a relatively unstructured, open-ended question is used, such as "How do you think of yourself politically?" some people would answer with "Democrat," "Republican," and so forth, but many others might give answers that were quite different, like "liberal," "conservative," "radical," "moderate," "pragmatic"—and these could not easily be compared with the partisan categories. Analysts often intend to force responses into a single dimension, such as partisanship, whether the respondents would have volunteered an answer along that dimension or not. This is essential if they are to develop single dimensions for analytic purposes. Modern survey research includes questions and techniques considerably more complex than these examples for establishing dimensions. A useful compilation of survey questions and indices from studies of political behavior is *Measures of Political Attitudes*[2] by Robinson, Rusk, and Head.

Interviewing

The selection of the sample depends in part on the interviewer, but even more important is the role of the interviewer in asking questions of the respondent and in recording the answers. Motivated, well-trained interviewers are crucial to the success of survey research. The interviewer has several major responsibilities: first is selection of the respondent according to sampling instructions. Second, the interviewer must develop rapport with the respondent so that he or she will be willing to go through with the interview, which may last an hour or more. Third, the interviewer must ask the questions in a friendly way and encourage the respondent to answer fully without distorting the answers. Finally, the interviewer must record the answers of the respondent fully and accurately. In order to accomplish these tasks with a high level of proficiency, a permanent staff of interviewers is trained and retrained by survey organizations.

Coding

Once the interviewers administer the questionnaires to respondents, the coders take over and reduce the verbal information to a numerical form according to a "code." Numeric information, unlike verbal information, can be processed and manipulated by high-speed, data-processing equipment. The coder's task may be simple or complex. For example, to code the respondent's sex requires a simple code:

1. Male
2. Female

A data card or magnetic tape that contains information on the respondent will have a location designated for indicating the respondent's sex. A value of "1" in this location will indicate male, and a value of

---

[2]John P. Robinson, Jerrold G. Rusk, and Kendra B. Head, *Measures of Political Attitudes* (Ann Arbor, Mich.: Institute for Social Research, 1968).

"2" will indicate female. The code shown above for partisan categories gives the numbers that would stand for various responses.

Some coding is very complicated with elaborate arrays of categories. For example, coding the responses to a question like "Is there anything in particular you like about the Democratic Party?" might include fifty or a hundred categories covering such details as "I like the party's farm policies," "I like the party's tax program," and "I've just always been a Democrat." Some codes require the coders to make judgments about the respondent's answers; in political surveys these codes have included judgments on the level of sophistication of the respondents' answers and judgments as to the main reason for respondents' vote choices. Sonquist and Dunkelberg treat question construction and coding in great detail in *Survey and Opinion Research*.[3]

After the coders have converted the verbal information into numbers according to the coding instructions, the numbers are entered in the computer and readied for analysis. At this point, the survey research process ends; the political analysts take over to make what use of the data they can.

Validity of Survey Questions

A frequent set of criticisms directed at public-opinion research questions the validity of the responses to survey items. Validity simply means the extent to which there is correspondence between the verbal response to a question and the actual attitude or behavior of the respondent that the question is designed to measure. There is no one answer to doubts about validity, since each item has a validity applicable to it alone. Some items are notoriously invalid; others have nearly perfect validity. Many survey items have not been independently tested for their validity, and for practical purposes, the researcher is forced to say that he is interested in analyzing the responses, whatever they mean to the respondent. In other instances the sample result can be compared with the known population value.

The items with the most questionable validity in political studies come from those situations in which respondents have some incentive to misrepresent the facts or when their memories may not be accurate.

---

[3]John A. Sonquist and William C. Dunkelberg, *Survey and Opinion Research* (Englewood Cliffs, N.J.: Prentice-Hall, 1977).

Questions about voting turnout or level of income are noteworthy in this regard, but validity checks reveal that respondents are about as likely to underestimate their income as overestimate it and about as likely to say they did not vote when in fact they did as to claim to have voted when they did not.

Recall of past voting behavior falls victim to failing memories and intervening events. Changes in party identification, past votes cast, the party identification of one's parents—all may contain substantial error. For example, during November and December immediately after the 1960 election, respondents were asked how they had voted for president. Most remembered voting for either Kennedy or Nixon, and, as shown in Table A–1, they were divided about evenly between the two. (The slight deviation of 1 percent from the actual results is within sampling error by any reasonable standards.) The 1962 and 1964 sample estimates of the 1960 vote reveal increasing departures from the actual outcome. Even granted that some change in the population over four years may affect vote-choice percentages, a substantial proportion of the 1964 sample gave responses to the question of 1960 presidential vote choice that misrepresented their actual vote. The validity of this item always declines over a four-year period, but Kennedy's assassination in the intervening years created an unusually large distortion in recalled vote.

A number of good texts on survey research methods are available. Two good introductions are Backstrom and Hursh-César's *Survey Research*[4] and Weisberg and Bowen's *An Introduction to Survey Re-*

TABLE A–1 Recalled Vote for President in 1960, 1962, and 1964

Reported Vote	1960	1962	1964
Kennedy	49%	56%	64%
Nixon	51	43	36
Other	*	*	*
Total	100%	99%	100%
n =	1428	940	1124

*less than 0.5 percent.

Source: Survey Research Center National Election Studies.

---

[4]Charles H. Backstrom and Gerald D. Hursh-César, *Survey Research*, 2nd ed. (New York: John Wiley & Sons, 1981).

search and Data Analysis.[5] The Survey Research Center has a *Manual for Interviewers* and a *Manual for Coders;*[6] these manuals provide a simple, thorough introduction to two phases of the data-collection process. Leslie Kish's *Survey Sampling*[7] is by far the most authoritative and difficult work on sampling. Kahn and Cannel have provided a description and defense of the Survey Research Center interviewing in *The Dynamics of Interviewing.*[8] All major survey research organizations can provide descriptions of their methods, but the best single collection of questionnaires, codes, and other methods from major political studies is available through the Inter-university Consortium for Political and Social Research located at the University of Michigan.

---

[5]Herbert F. Weisberg and Bruce D. Bowen, *An Introduction to Survey Research and Data Analysis* (San Francisco: W. H. Freeman and Co., 1977).

[6]These manuals are available from the Survey Research Center at the University of Michigan, Ann Arbor, Michigan.

[7]Leslie Kish, *Survey Sampling* (New York: John Wiley & Sons, 1965).

[8]Robert Kahn and Charles Cannel, *The Dynamics of Interviewing* (New York: John Wiley & Sons, 1957).

APPENDIX B

Aggregate Election Statistics

During recent decades, when survey research archives have received major attention from social scientists, there has been a considerable but less visible effort to establish archives of election statistics and other historical records. The major enterprise in this area is the Historical Archive of the Inter-university Consortium for Political and Social Research, which has acquired a number of data collections including congressional roll calls from 1787 to the present, census data for states and counties since 1790, and county-level election returns for major offices. From the Historical Archive, students of electoral history can receive data for presidential, gubernatorial, Senate, and House elections by states and by counties, including the party designation and the total votes for each candidate. This archive is virtually complete for all states from 1824 or from statehood to the present. Of course, all sorts of election data are also available in state and local government documents.

Basic Political Indicators

For much electoral analysis, the creation of indicators is fairly simple. The most commonly used variable is the party's percentage of the total vote, which can be calculated for each candidate, and, of course, such percentages can be calculated for many races. Some other commonly needed variables pose more problems. Turnout indicators usually are calculated by using the total number of voters divided by the eligible electorate, but under many circumstances the eligible electorate is difficult to estimate and is rarely known as accurately as the total vote. As discussed in Chapter 4, aggregate indicators of the "normal vote" or underlying party strength are extremely useful in the analysis of electoral change over time and as a baseline for interpreting the outcomes in specific elections. These indicators are usually composite indices based on votes from several races or averaging votes in a single race over several elections. Occasionally a single race, often of low visibility, is chosen on the assumption that the lack of information on the candidates or issues will cause voters to make their choices on the basis of long-term partisan preferences. Inevitably, these indicators are somewhat arbitrary in the selection of elements and in their weighting, and none is as satisfactory as Converse's measurement of the normal vote based on survey data.[1] On the other hand, the concept is so crucial for electoral analysis, attempts to create good estimates of it from aggregate data will doubtless continue.[2]

These variables are usually well-behaved, interval measures to which a far greater variety of statistical techniques can be applied with confidence than is true of survey data. These simple data are ordinarily free of serious errors and usually are complete, since they are official statistics. The percentage of the vote and turnout indicators have face validity, although the same cannot be said for the various indicators of underlying party strength.[3]

Inference with Aggregate Data

The enthusiasm for survey research in recent years has sometimes created the impression that election returns and census data are less useful and less valuable for political analysis. To be sure, there are

---

[1]Philip E. Converse, "The Concept of a Normal Vote," in Angus Campbell et al., *Elections and the Political Order* (New York: John Wiley & Sons, 1966), pp. 9–39.

[2]A collection of such estimates for all states is found in Paul T. David, *Party Strength in the United States: 1872–1970* (Charlottesville: University Press of Virginia, 1972).

[3]For a discussion of various indicators used with aggregate electoral data, see William H. Flanigan and Nancy H. Zingale, "Summarizing Quantitative Data" in *Analyzing Electoral History: A Guide to the Study of American Voter Behavior,*

many disadvantages and difficulties in aggregate data that should not be minimized. Probably the most important of these—and certainly the most notorious—is the danger in making inferences about individual behavior from information about aggregated units.[4] For example, we know that the counties with high percentages of Catholics also tend to be the most Democratic counties. We cannot validly conclude that Catholics as individuals are the ones who are voting Democratic without individual-level data. Since analysts often are interested in individual-level relationships, temptation to violate the rules of inference and discuss individual behavior when only aggregate relationships are known is widespread. On the other hand, there are still many interesting topics that deal with the behavior of aggregated groups, such as state electorates, and aggregate data is the appropriate material to use for such analysis.

Historical election statistics have other important, if obvious, advantages over survey data. These are the only data available for study over long periods in the past, and, for analysis within limited geographical areas even in the present time, aggregate data are all that are available. Unfortunately, election statistics and census data offer a narrow range of information, and they do not include the rich and varied indicators needed for most political analysis, such as political attitudes, patterns of past and present individual voting behavior, and intensities of political preferences. Analysts used to having survey data find it particularly frustrating to face the severe substantive limitations of historical aggregate data analysis

Problems with Aggregate Data in Over-time Analysis

Many of the problems with aggregate data are present only in over-time analysis, not in cross-sectional analysis. Cross-sectional analysis examines the relationship among variables across a set of units at one point in time, whereas over-time analysis considers a single unit at several points of time. Problems of comparability can arise with even the simplest of indicators viewed across time. For example, in a series

---

ed. Jerome M. Clubb, William H. Flanigan, and Nancy H. Zingale (Beverly Hills, Calif.: Sage Publications, 1981), pp. 228–233.

[4]For the most authoritative discussion of inference problems with aggregate data, see Gudmund R. Iversen, "Group Data and Individual Data" in Clubb, Flanigan, and Zingale (eds.), *Analyzing Electoral History*, pp. 267–302.

of elections, the candidates for a particular office change quite often, so the name of the candidate is not a basis for organizing a set of percentages for a party. At first it seems no problem to use the party label in place of the candidate's name, but this is not the case. Party labels change over the years, sometimes parties split briefly and then reunite, and in some circumstances candidates run under several party labels. The analyst must decide how to organize such data in a single series. The analyst must decide what to include and exclude under a particular party label over the years. In the past one hundred and fifty years, about one thousand party labels have been used in major elections alone.

Geographical Units

There may be other data problems in election series. For example, units may change over the years. State legislative districts, congressional districts, and precincts are extremely likely to change boundaries, although states are unlikely to change. County boundaries are currently quite stable, but in earlier years in most states considerable redrawing of existing county lines occurred as new counties were organized. Lack of continuity in geographical units makes analysis of historical changes a hazardous undertaking.

Another set of problems with geographical units arises when an attempt is made to merge census and election data. There are no extraordinary difficulties in merging data from states and counties, although census variables will usually need to be interpolated to create values for all election years. For smaller units, like census tracts and precincts, merging is always imperfect and quite arbitrary. Such merging is relatively acceptable because adjacent units of either type are so often similar in behavior that the poor fit of boundaries does not lead to mistaken estimates of their characteristics.

Geographical units pose another problem in analysis. They are almost invariably of different sizes in terms of population, numbers of voters, and so forth. For some estimates, weighted data are used so that the total values of subunits of varying sizes will sum to the proper value for the whole unit.

Election data have extraordinary advantages over survey research for the political analyst. They are widely available and not expensive to collect for analysis. Few scholars can afford to direct a public opinion survey, although more have access to the data archives of surveys originally conducted by someone else. But limited amounts of election and census data can be compiled and handled inexpensively and fairly conveniently, even without a computer.

A bibliographic guide to printed sources of national, state, and local election data is found in *Analyzing Electoral History*, edited by Clubb, Flanigan, and Zingale, as well as chapters on methodological issues in aggregate analysis such as demographic and boundary changes and combining census with election data. The methodological literature on analysis of election data is not extensive, but V. O. Key's *A Primer of Statistics for Political Scientists*[5] is a good introduction to the subject.

---

[5]V. O. Key, *A Primer of Statistics for Political Scientists* (New York: Thomas Y. Crowell Co., 1959).

Index

$$\star \star \star$$

ABC/Washington Post Poll, 191
Abortion, attitude toward, 95,
    104–106
Abramson, Paul, xiii, 23, 82, 84
Age:
    and attitudes, 104–106, 108–110,
        182, 185–186
    and partisan change, 81–91
    and turnout, 18–20, 22
Agenda setting, 153
Aggregate election data, 199–203
Aldrich, John H., xiii, 23
Alford, Robert, 64
Alienation, 16–17 (see also
    Cynicism)
Almond, Gabriel, 178
Amendments, constitutional, 2–4, 6,
    8
American Enterprise Institute, xiv
American Independent Party, 27
American Party, 27
Andersen, Kristi, 80, 113
Anderson, John, 26–27, 34, 43–44,
    124
Andrews, William, 9

Apter, David, 95, 112
Asher, Herbert, xii
Attitude change, 147–154
    and mass media, 157–165
Attitudes (see also Issues):
    toward domestic economic policy,
        99–102, 138–139, 142–144
    toward foreign policy, 98,
        106–110, 114, 136–138,
        142–144
    toward social and racial policy,
        102–106
Attitudinal cross-pressure, 67–68,
    148–150
Australian ballot, 12

Backstrom, Charles, 196
Barber, James, 165
Beatty, Kathleen M., xiv
Beck, Paul, xv, 87–88, 103, 182
Berelson, Bernard, x, 65, 67
Bishop, George, 113
Blacks, 54, 58, 60
    nonvoting, 20–22
    registration of, 5–7, 60

suffrage and disfranchisement, 2–8, 10, 15
Bogue, Allan, 5
Born-again Christians, 60–61
Bowen, Bruce, 196–197
Boyd, Richard, 134
Brodbeck, A. J., xiv
Brody, Richard, 134, 136
Brown, Thad, xi, 180
Bruner, Jere, 87–88, 103, 182
Bryan, William Jennings, 77
Budge, Ian, 29
Bull Moose Party, 27
Burdick, Eugene, xiv
Bureau of Applied Social Research, x, 44, 65
Bureau of the Census, 7, 9, 38, 71–72, 79
Burnham, W. Dean, xiv, 9–11, 75
Butler, David, 64, 82
Byrd, Harry, 27

Campaigns, 154–170
    participation, 154–157
    spending, 15–16
    strategy, 168–170
Campbell, Angus, vii, xi, 11, 13, 26, 28–29, 40–42, 55–56, 58–60, 64, 70, 111–112, 142, 200
Candidate image, 122–128, 142–143
Cannel, Charles, 197
Carter, Jimmy, 22, 59–61, 79, 124, 126–128, 130, 140, 142, 144–145, 159, 161–165, 181
Catholics, 50, 58, 60, 100 (see also Religion)
CBS/New York Times Poll, 191
Center for Political Studies, vii–viii, xi–xiv, 19, 30, 33, 45–46, 49, 53, 61, 80, 83, 89–90, 101–102, 105, 108, 113, 115, 117–118, 127, 135, 138–139, 160, 164, 180, 182, 186, 189, 192 (see also Survey Research Center)
Chambers, William, 75

Childhood socialization (see Socialization)
Citizenship training, 3 (see also Socialization)
Citrin, Jack, 181
Civic duty, 18, 178–179
Civil liberties (see Democratic values)
Civil rights (see Issues)
Clausen, Aage, xi
Clubb, Jerome, xiv, 11, 71–73, 201, 203
Coding, 194–195
Coercion, 17–18
Cognitive dissonance (see Dissonance)
Cohen, Bernard, 153
Cohort analysis, 82–83, 88–91
Communication, political, 147–148, 150–154 (see also Mass media)
Compartmentalization, 149
Competitiveness, 10–11, 15, 33, 39, 74–78, 91
Conformity, 57
Congressional elections:
    turnout, 13–14, 40–42
    voting in, 36–42, 44, 78–79
Consensus (see Democratic values)
Conservatism, 10, 110–111, 114–117
Constitutional amendments (see Amendments, constitutional)
Constitutional Union Party, 27
Converse, Philip, xi, xiii, 11, 26, 55, 81–82, 84, 95, 112–113, 160–161, 200
Coombs, Steven, 159
Corruption, 11–12
Crewe, Ivor, xv, 29
Crew, Robert, 64
Crocket, H. J., 173
Cross-pressure, 65–68 (see also Attitudinal cross-pressure)
Cynicism, 17

Daley, Richard, 132
Dalton, Russell J., xv

David, Paul T., 200
Dealignment, 74
Democratic Party, 47, 75, 116, 129, 131–132
  vote for, 27, 38, 43–44, 46, 71, 76–81
Democratic values, 172–179, 186–187
Democrats, 52–55, 59–60, 84, 86–89, 91 (*see also* Partisans)
Demonstrations, 184–187
Dennis, Everette E., 153, 159
Dennis, Jack, 176, 178
Denver, David, xv
Deviating election, 70, 73–74
Directive opinion, 94
Dissonance, 149–150
Dobson, Douglas, 87–88, 103, 182
Domestic economic policy (*see* Attitudes toward domestic economic policy; Issues)
Downs, Anthony, xiii
Dunkelberg, William, 195

Eagleton, Thomas, 125
Easton, David, 176, 178
Ecological inference, 200–201
Education, 49–51
  and attitudes, 95, 100–101, 104–106, 113, 116–117, 185
  levels of, 18, 21
  relation to turnout, 18–20, 22
  and socialization, 176–179
Efficacy, sense of political, 23, 171, 182–184
Eighteen-year-old vote, 3–4, 7–8, 18
Eisenhower, Dwight, 26, 34, 42, 70, 122–123, 166, 168
Elections (*see* Congressional elections; Presidential elections)
Enfranchisement (*see* Suffrage)
Epstein, Laurily K., 22
Erikson, Robert S., 80–81
Expected vote, 70–72, 77, 200

Family socialization (*see* Socialization)
Farlie, Dennis, 29
Federalist Party, 75
Feldman, Jacob, 164
Ferraro, Geraldine, 127, 145
Festinger, Leon, 149
Fiorina, Morris P., xiv, 140
Flanagan, Scott, xv
Flanigan, William H., xiv, 5, 11, 64, 70–73, 200–201, 203
Ford, Gerald, 61, 124–126, 159, 164–165
Foreign policy (*see* Attitudes toward foreign policy; Issues)
Franchise (*see* Suffrage)
Free Soil Party, 27
Fundamentalists, 60–61

Gallup, George, 30, 43
Gallup Poll, 80, 109
Gatekeeping, 153
Gaudet, Hazel, x, 65
Generational change, 81, 86–88
Goldwater, Barry, 26, 34, 42, 123, 130, 134, 142
Grenada, 153
Gurin, Gerald, xi, 28

Habitual nonvoters, 20–22
Hadley, Arthur T., 17
Hagner, Paul R., xiv, 111–112
Hart, Gary, 127
Head, Kendra, 194
Hess, Robert, 176–178
High-stimulus elections, 13
Hinckley, Barbara, 39–40
Historical election analysis, 199–203
Hostage crisis in Iran, 98, 110, 126, 142, 152
Humphrey, Hubert H., 59, 126, 136–137
Hursh-César, Gerald, 196

Ideological self-identificaaon, 115–119

Ideology, 93, 110–119 (*see also* Conservatism; Liberalism)
Immigrants, 5, 7
Incumbency, 37, 39–40
Independents, 30–33, 42–47, 52–55, 74, 80–88
Information, 11, 13, 16–18, 66, 95, 160, 162
Institute for Social Research, vii, xi
Integration (*see* Issues)
Interest in politics, 11, 13, 15–20, 41–42, 46–47, 66, 95, 159–160
Inter-university Consortium for Political and Social Research, vii–viii, xi–xii, xiv–xv, 14, 27, 87–88, 103, 189, 197, 199
Interviewing, 194
Involvement (*see* Interest in politics)
Iran (*see* Hostage crisis in Iran)
Issue constraint, 112–115
Issues, 94–110, 112–114, 118 (*see also* Attitudes)
 abortion, 95, 104–106
 economic, 98–102, 138–139
 foreign aid, 109
 integration, 102–103
 military spending, 109–110, 137–138
 prayer in the schools, 104
 Vietnam, 95, 98, 106–110
 and vote choice, 132–144
Iversen, Gudmund, 201

Jackson, Andrew, 75
Jackson, Jesse, 60
Jeffersonian Republicans, 75–76
Jennings, M. Kent, xiii, 84–87, 182, 186
Jews, 49, 54, 58, 100 (*see also* Religion)
Johnson, Lyndon B., 26, 42, 107, 123, 134

Kahn, Robert, 197
Katz, Elihu, 150, 164
Kennedy, Edward, 161–162

Kennedy, John F., 27, 60, 122–123, 125, 157, 163–164, 175, 196
Kessel, John, 134
Key, V. O., Jr., xii, xiv, 70, 203
Kirkpatrick, Jeane, 175
Kish, Leslie, 197
Kousser, J. Morgan, 5
Kovenock, David, 64
Kraus, Sidney, 164

Lane, Robert E., 9
Lang, Gladys, 125
Lang, Kurt, 125
Lazarsfeld, Paul, x, 65, 67, 150
Lebanon, 153
Legal restrictions on suffrage (*see* Suffrage)
Levels of conceptualization, 111–112
Levitin, Teresa, 83
Liberalism, 110–111, 114–118
Life-cycle effect, 81–86
Linquiti, Peter, 22
Lipset, Seymour M., xv, 76
Literacy tests, 2, 5
Low-stimulus elections, 13, 18

McClosky, Herbert, 173–174
McClure, Robert, 158, 163
McGovern, George, 26, 59, 123–126, 134–136, 163
MacKuen, Michael, 159
McPhee, William, x, 65, 67
Manipulation, 11, 16–18
Marcus, George, 113, 173
Markus, Gregory B., 85, 113
Mass media, 13, 15, 125–128, 147, 150–154
 and attitude change, 157–165, 168–169
 and turnout, 22–23
Matthews, Donald, 5
Middle class (*see* Social classes)
Miller, Arthur, xi–xii, 45, 123, 142–143, 180–181

Miller, Warren, vii, xi–xii, 28, 37, 55, 83, 123, 134, 136, 142
Minor parties (*see* Third-party candidates)
Mondale, Walter F., 42, 60, 79, 124, 127, 136–139, 144–145, 162, 164
Mueller, John E., 106
Munger, Frank, xiv

National Opinion Research Center, xiii, 30, 99, 109, 173
National Republican Party, 27
NBC Poll, 191
New Deal (*see* Realignment)
Niemi, Richard, xii–xiii, 84, 142–143, 182, 186
Nie, Norman, xii–xiii, 80, 112–113, 134, 141
Nimmo, Dan, 125
Nixon, Richard M., 26, 59, 70, 108–109, 122–124, 126–127, 134–137, 157, 163–164, 175, 181, 196
Nonvoting, 16–24
Normal vote, 26 (*see also* Expected vote)
North, 6, 31
    decline of turnout in, 10–12
Nunn, C. Z., 173

Occupation, 49–50
Occupational mobility (*see* Social mobility)
Oldendick, Robert, 113
Opinion change (*see* Attitude change)
Opinion leadership, 150–151
Ordeshook, Peter, xiii

Page, Benjamin, xiv, 127, 134, 136
Participation (*see* Campaigns, participation; Turnout)
Partisan loyalty (*see* Partisanship)
Partisan realignment (*see* Realignment)

Partisans, 29–33, 45, 74, 130, 154, 156, 160, 162–163 (*see also* Democrats; Republicans)
    and ideology, 115–116
    and issues, 98, 100–102, 107–109
    political characteristics of, 33–42, 46
    social characteristics of, 49–55
Partisanship, 25–55, 130, 141
    change in, 69–91
    concept of, 26, 28–29, 69
    decline in, 23, 25
    defections from, 34–37
    issues, 96–98, 101–103
    party identification, measurement of, 25–37, 44–45
    and social class, 62–64
    stability of, 11, 25–26, 29
    strength of, 28–29, 40, 81
Party campaign activities (*see* Campaigns)
Party identification (*see* Partisanship)
Party image, 128–132
Party system, 74–78
Patterson, Thomas, 158–160, 162–163, 165
People's Party, 27 (*see also* Populists)
Period effect, 81
Permissive opinions, 94
Petrocik, John, xii, 47, 80, 112, 134, 141–142
Pierce, John, xiii-xiv, 111–112, 141, 173
Piereson, James, 113, 173
Political Action Committees, 128, 156
Political culture, 3, 171–175, 186
Political efficacy (*see* Efficacy, sense of political)
Political socialization (*see* Socialization)
Poll tax, 5–6
Pomper, Gerald, xii, 98, 134
Populists, 77

Presidential elections:
  turnout, 9, 13–15, 17–19, 21–22,
    40–42, 44
  voting in, 26–27, 33–34, 37,
    40–44, 46, 56, 58–62, 71–72,
    121–146, 196
Prewitt, Kenneth, 173
Primary elections, 13, 18, 40–41, 162
  white primary, 5
Primary groups, 55–57
Progressive Party, 27
Property requirements, 2, 7
Protestants, 50, 59–61 (see also
  Religion)
Prothro, James, 5, 64
Public opinion, 93–110 (see also
  Attitudes; Issues)
Public financing of campaigns,
  15–16

Questionnaire construction, 192–194

Race, 49–51, 53–55, 78, 100–102,
  116–117, 180–182 (see also
  Blacks)
Raine, Alden, xi, 180
Ranney, Austin, 18
Rationalization, 150
Reagan, Ronald, 22, 25, 34, 42, 60,
  79, 88, 91, 97, 100, 110–111,
  124, 128, 130, 134, 136–139,
  142, 144–145, 153, 162–165,
  181, 184
Realignment, 25, 47, 69, 73–81, 88,
  91, 96–97
  Civil War realignment, 73, 75–76,
    80–81, 132
  New Deal realignment, 73, 77–78,
    84, 96–98, 100
  realignment of 1896, 73, 77
Reference group, 58, 60 (see also
  Secondary groups)
Region (see also North; South):
  alignments based on, 75–79
  differences in attitudes, 100–101,
    103, 117

differences in partisanship, 29,
    31–33, 49–55, 59–64
  differences in turnout, 9, 12–13,
    21
Registration, 5–6, 12, 20, 60
Religion, 49–51, 53–55, 59–61,
  65–66, 100–101, 104–106,
  116–117 (see also Catholics;
  Jews; Protestants)
RePass, David, 139
Republican Party, 47, 116, 129, 131
  vote for, 27, 38, 43–44, 72, 76–78
Republicans, 52–55, 82, 84, 87–88
  90–91 (see also Partisans)
Residence requirements, 2, 6, 12
Riker, William, xiii
Robinson, John, 194
Rohde, David W., xiii
Rokkan, Stein, xv, 76
Roosevelt, Franklin D., 168
Roosevelt, Theodore, 26, 77
Rosenberg, Milton, 149
Rosenstone, Steven J., 12
Rose, Richard, 64
Rules of the game (see Democratic
  values)
Rusk, Jerrold, xi, 5, 11, 194

Sampling, 190–192
Schattschneider, E. E., 10
Schmitz, John G., 43
Schneider, Edward J., xii, 123
Secondary groups, 55, 57–62
Selective exposure, 149, 163
Selective perception, 149
Sense of political efficacy (see
  Efficacy)
Shanks, Merrill, 134, 136, 142
Shortridge, Ray M., 11
Short-term forces, 26, 39, 121–122,
  140–144
Silbey, Joel, 5
Single-issue voting, 132–133
Social classes, 49–50, 52, 55, 62–64,
  65–66, 77–78, 95, 178
Social groups (see Secondary groups)

Socialization, 3, 18, 86–88, 176–179
Social mobility, 64
Sonquist, John, 195
South, 2–4, 29, 32–33, 50, 54, 61 (*see also* Region)
  disfranchisement of blacks in, 2, 5–8, 10, 15
  nonvoting, 20–22
  turnout, 6
Southern Democratic Party, 27
Stevenson, Adlai, 26, 122, 166
Stokes, Donald, xi, 37, 55, 64, 82, 142
Stouffer, Samuel, 173
Strom, Gerald, 22
Stucker, John, 5
Suffrage, 1–8
  extensions of, 2–4, 6–8, 10, 18
  property requirements, 2, 7
  restrictions on, 1–2, 4–8
Sullivan, John, xiii, 113, 141, 173
Sundquist, James, xiv
Supreme Court, 6
Surge and decline, 40–42
Survey Research Center, vii, x–xii, 28, 30, 44, 49, 68, 98, 107, 112, 189–190, 192–193, 196–197
Survey Research Center/Center for Political Studies, 21, 32, 35–36, 43–45, 51, 63, 107–108, 155, 167, 183, 185 (*see also* Center for Political Studies)
Survey research methods, 94–95, 189–198
System support, 179–187

Tedin, Kent L., 80–81
Television, 152–153, 159–160 (*see also* Mass media)
  debates, 157, 159, 163–164
Third-party candidates, 26, 44, 75, 77
Ticket splitting, 11, 34, 66
Time of vote decision, 166–168
Torney, Judith, 176–178
Truman, Harry S., 130

Trust in government, 171, 180–182, 184
Tuchfarber, Alfred, 113
Turnout, 1, 8–24, 40–42, 46–47
  calculation of turnout rate, 8–9, 200
  decline in, 10–12, 15, 18, 22–24
Two-step flow of communication, 150–151

Udall, Morris, 165
Union members, 58–60

Validity of survey questions, 195–196
Verba, Sidney, xii–xiii, 80, 112, 134, 141, 173, 178
Vietnam, 95, 98, 106–110, 114, 116, 133–137, 140, 152
Violence, 5–6, 184–187
Vote choice, 121–146
  and issues, 132–146
Voter registration (*see* Registration)
Voting Rights Act, 6

Wallace, George, 26, 33, 43–44, 124, 136–137
Watergate, 130, 152, 180–181
Wattenberg, Martin P., 45, 142–143
Weisberg, Herbert, xii–xiii, 142–143, 196–197
Whig Party, 27, 75, 132
Williams, J. A., 173
Williamson, Chilton, 2
Wolfe, Arthur, xi
Wolfinger, Raymond E., 12, 22
Women:
  suffrage, 2–4, 7–8
  turnout, 20–22
Working class (*see* Social classes)

Young people (*see* Age)

Zingale, Nancy H., xiv, 11, 70–73, 200–201, 203